"*Our Father's World* is a beautiful and inspiring book. I will keep it on hand both for consultation and reference. When I first opened it, the question on my mind was, 'Will evangelicals read it?' As I approached the close, the question became 'Will secular environmentalists read it?' They need to read it and understand the power Christianity has to help save the living environment—not just in voting numbers but also out of strength from spirituality and rational argument."

E. O. WILSON, HARVARD UNIVERSITY, AUTHOR OF *CONSILIENCE* AND *THE CREATION: AN APPEAL TO SAVE LIFE ON EARTH*

"*Our Father's World* brings an important international perspective from one who has spent a lifetime involved in evangelical missionary efforts. . . . Brown marshals arguments from Scripture to persuade Christian readers that environmental stewardship should have been part of the mission of the church all along."

ANDY CROUCH, IN *BOOKS & CULTURE*

"This is an important book that should be on every pastor's shelf and in every church library. Creation today is crying out for the church to begin preaching and practicing the full biblical message of stewardship."

JOSEPH K. SHELDON, PROFESSOR OF BIOLOGY AND ENVIRONMENTAL SCIENCE, MESSIAH COLLEGE

"This book is a remarkable combination of a broad spectrum of the environmental crisis in the world today coupled with a deep understanding of God's desire for his creation as developed in the Scriptures. It is full of well-written illustrations that show what the church (universal) and the church (local) need to do to obey God's commands and desires for his world. I highly recommend this book as both easily readable yet profound in its challenge to Christians and others today."

DAVID M. HOWARD, FORMER PRESIDENT, LATIN AMERICA MISSION

"*Our Father's World* helps identify some of the most pressing moral questions of our age: Is there an environmental crisis? If there is, why should we care and what should we do about it? Turning to the living Bible for answers, Ed Brown helps church leaders become better stewards of God's creation. A valuable addition to the growing creation-care movement, *Our Father's World* offers a message of hope and redemption: 'though the wrong seems oft so strong, God is the ruler yet.'"

J. MATTHEW SLEETH, M.D., AUTHOR OF *SERVE GOD, SAVE THE PLANET*, AND EXECUTIVE DIRECTOR, A ROCHA USA

"*Our Father's World* offers a marvelous contribution to the evangelical creation-care movement. The book is simultaneously intellectual and practical. The first half of the book offers a rather comprehensive recasting of core biblical theology themes in a remarkably accessible way. It shows the potential for mainstreaming creation-care concerns into evangelical theology, which is crucial for the future of creation care among us. The second half of the book turns in a very practical direction, offering a thoughtful and thorough treatment of action steps for Christian care of creation. What I most appreciate about the book is Brown's recognition that ultimately the crisis in God's creation is a spiritual problem, a failure to live rightly before and with God and neighbor, and therefore it requires a profoundly spiritual solution. This means that the church, more than the state, holds the key to the human future. An excellent book."

DAVID P. GUSHEE, DISTINGUISHED UNIVERSITY PROFESSOR OF CHRISTIAN ETHICS, MCAFEE SCHOOL OF THEOLOGY, AND PRESIDENT, EVANGELICALS FOR HUMAN RIGHTS

"*Our Father's World* clearly lays out how mistreatment of the physical world around us is the result of sin, how care of God's creation is a biblical mandate and how the church, the corporate body of believers around the world, can bring about significant change. The issues this book addresses are vitally important for Christians today."

JIM TEBBE, DIRECTOR OF THE URBANA STUDENT MISSIONS CONVENTION AND VICE PRESIDENT OF MISSIONS, INTERVARSITY CHRISTIAN FELLOWSHIP

OUR FATHER'S WORLD

MOBILIZING THE CHURCH TO CARE FOR CREATION

EDWARD R. BROWN

IVP Books

An imprint of InterVarsity Press
Downers Grove, Illinois

InterVarsity Press
P.O. Box 1400, Downers Grove, IL 60515-1426
World Wide Web: www.ivpress.com
E-mail: email@ivpress.com

1st edition ©2006 by Edward R. Brown
2nd edition ©2008 by Edward R. Brown

InterVarsity Press® is the book-publishing division of InterVarsity Christian Fellowship/USA®, a student movement active on campus at hundreds of universities, colleges and schools of nursing in the United States of America, and a member movement of the International Fellowship of Evangelical Students. For information about local and regional activities, write Public Relations Dept., InterVarsity Christian Fellowship/USA, 6400 Schroeder Rd., P.O. Box 7895, Madison, WI 53707-7895, or visit the IVCF website at <www.intervarsity.org>.

All Scripture quotations, unless otherwise indicated, are taken from the Holy Bible, New International Version®. NIV®. Copyright ©1973, 1978, 1984 by International Bible Society. Used by permission of Zondervan Publishing House. All rights reserved.

Excerpt from The Lorax by Dr. Seuss ™ and © by Dr. Seuss Enterprises, L.P. 1971, renewed 1999. Used by permission of Random House Children's Books, a division of Random House, Inc.

Design: Janelle Rebel
Images: iStockphoto

ISBN 978-0-8308-3484-6

Printed in the United States of America ∞

 green press INITIATIVE InterVarsity Press is committed to protecting the environment and to the responsible use of natural resources. As a member of the Green Press Initiative we use recycled paper whenever possible. To learn more about the Green Press Initiative, visit http://www.greenpressinitiative.org

Library of Congress Cataloging-in-Publication Data

Brown, Edward R. (Edward Ralph)
  Our Father's world: mobilizing the church to care for creation /
Edward R. Brown.
    p. cm.
  Includes bibliographical references (p.   ).
  ISBN 978-0-8308-3484-6 (pbk.: alk. paper)
  1. Human ecology—Religious aspects—Christianity. 2. Stewardship.
Christian. 3. Nature—Religious aspects—Christianity. I. Title.
  BT695.5.B755 2008
  261.8'8—dc22

                                                                2008002180

P   19   18   17   16   15   14   13   12   11   10   9   8   7   6   5   4   3   2   1
Y   24   23   22   21   20   19   18   17   16   15   14   13   12   11   10   09   08

For Susanna, my Rafiq-i-Hayat

This is my Father's world,
and to my listening ears
all nature sings, and round me rings
the music of the spheres.
This is my Father's world:
I rest me in the thought
of rocks and trees, of skies and seas;
his hand the wonders wrought.

This is my Father's world,
the birds their carols raise,
the morning light, the lily white,
declare their maker's praise.
This is my Father's world:
he shines in all that's fair;
in the rustling grass I hear him pass;
he speaks to me everywhere.

This is my Father's world.
O let me ne'er forget
that though the wrong seems oft so strong,
God is the ruler yet.
This is my Father's world:
why should my heart be sad?
The Lord is King; let the heavens ring!
God reigns; let the earth be glad!

Maltbie D. Babcock, 1901

Contents

Foreword

I am privileged to write the foreword for this most important book. Ed Brown is a remarkable follower of Christ and a respected servant-leader in the evangelical environmental world. Like many of us, his commitment to solving the crises documented in this book is exceeded only by his love of his family and of the Lord, for whom we have committed the rest of our lives to creation-care service.

I am moved by the first two lines of the third stanza of "My Father's World": "This is my Father's world. Oh let me ne'er forget." My brothers and sisters in Christ, we forgot. Our material progress in the so-called developed countries has too often come at the price of the "least of these," and now the impending price of the planet on which we depend upon for our very existence.

I recently returned from the Intergovernmental Panel on Climate Change as the only observer representing a Christian organization. I am more convinced than ever that while debates may go on about the causes of climate change, the IPCC studies and global negotiations on limiting greenhouse gases have two fundamental flaws. First, while there is an important role for governments, politicians will not solve the issues this book raises. Second, greenhouse gas reductions are necessary but not sufficient to stabilize and restore the planet's health. The solutions ultimately lie in changed lives for Christ, yours and mine, that will inspire and ripple through our families, vocations, communities, regions, countries and planet.

Ed Brown is right. Current scientific evidence of planetary degradation, from the most widely researched and peer-reviewed analysis in the history of our world, is our clear Macedonian call to awareness, reflection, prayer and action. Many of us believe we only have a ten-year window to address the growing crisis both in the climate system and in the rest of the biosphere before the consequences begin to multiply exponentially. This book makes a clear case for how we as Christians can and must mobilize our churches to meet that challenge.

Ed Brown makes the case for why the church is the last, best hope for response to this defining issue of the twenty-first century. As we now learn to preach widely the theology of creation care, how will churches stand up to the scrutiny of "how now shall churches live" creation care–committed lives? Will churches serve as inspiring examples to their members and communities alike?

Our Father's World is our clarion call. If we hear its prophetic voice and respond collectively as pastors and laity, united in our commitment to move toward the goal of leaving the planet in better shape than each generation inherited it, only then may it be said, "Well done, thou good and faithful stewards of his creation!"

Dr. Ed Johnson
President
Au Sable Institute for Environmental Studies
Grand Rapids, Michigan

Introduction

"Sometimes you just have to leap, and build your wings on the way down."

That was the heading on a letter I sent to friends and family in April 2005. Recently unemployed, I was explaining why my wife and I were embarking on an effort to form a new evangelical environmental missions organization. It didn't seem like a very rational decision—it wasn't!—and we were terrified. But Susanna and I believed we were following God's guidance. More than that, we believed we had a new perspective in our response to the environmental crisis that others needed to be aware of, for we had come to believe that the whole church of Jesus Christ and the ordinary people who are its members are the best and perhaps the only hope for a true solution to the global environmental crisis.

It all started with an e-mail message from Kenya: "How would you like to help us?"

You may be familiar with an incident in the Bible sometimes referred to as "the Macedonian call." In Acts 16, the apostle Paul and a group traveling with him were unsure of where God wanted them to go next in their mission of sharing the good news about Jesus Christ. Paul had a dream of a man from Macedonia, a Roman province across the Aegean Sea from northern Turkey, where the party was at the time. "Come over to Macedonia and help us," said the man (v. 9).

In my case, it was December 2004. I was sitting at my computer, very much awake. But the appeal in that e-mail could have been lifted right out of the pages of the New Testament. A missionary in Kenya was saying, "We need to start a new missions organization. Why don't you help us?"

Craig Sorley grew up in East Africa. He loves God and Africa, and he has a passion for caring for God's world. I had known Craig for a couple of years, and I had been following his efforts to establish an "environmental missions" project near Nairobi, watching him work to hold back a massive environmental crisis that has seen large parts of his childhood homeland suffer devastation and destruction on an unbelievable scale. Craig had tried and been unable to find a missions organization working in Kenya that was willing to take his project and his environmental vision under its wing.

I was Chief Operating Officer for Au Sable Institute, a Christian environmental organization. My position was about to disappear due to restructuring. My wife and I had been wrestling with what our future would be. Unemployment when you're over fifty, with three college-age children and no money in the bank is not a pleasant prospect, but starting a brand-new organization that's both evangelical and environmental is just crazy—sort of like walking on water. It would take that much faith and more.

In spite of all that, Craig's invitation was intriguing and even tempting, for I agreed with his premise that the church of Jesus Christ is the key to environmental healing. His message, "We want to transform people *and* the land they live on," went to my heart.

You'd have to call me a reluctant environmentalist. In twenty-five-plus years of Christian ministry, I've had a wide range of experience. At one time or another, I've been a pastor, a campus minister for international students, a missionary, a missions administrator, a chief operating officer and recently a country director for a Christian development organization responding to the Pakistan earthquake of 2005. I certainly have learned how to write resumés! But even with all this variety, I would never have predicted that I would find myself starting an environmental missions organization.

I had spent the previous five years working with Calvin DeWitt, founder of Au Sable Institute and someone many consider to be the father of the modern evangelical environmental movement in North America. Though my responsibilities were not directly related to the science program, I had the privilege of working closely with faculty members and students from more than sixty Christian colleges from around the country. I was able to meet and learn from Sir Ghillian Prance, an Au Sable board member and one of the foremost horticultural experts in the world, and Sir John Houghton, then head of the Intergovernmental Panel on Climate Change (IPCC), with whom Au Sable collaborated in organizing an international climate conference in Oxford, England, in the summer of 2005. Among the guests at that conference were the Reverend Jim Ball of the Evangelical Environmental Network, soon to become known for his "What Would Jesus Drive?" campaign, and the Reverend Richard Cizik of the National Association of Evangelicals. Because of that conference, Cizik would become one of the most outspoken evangelical proponents of environmental action in the United States, particularly with regard to climate change. And there were regular breakfast meetings with DeWitt, during which I was able to absorb a measure of his passion and a tiny portion of his knowledge concerning the state of God's creation today.

It was an eventful five years—and it transformed my perspective on God, his creation and the urgency of the environmental crisis facing the world today. I was becoming convinced that the answer to the environmental crisis is not with scientists. Science has made tremendous progress since Earth Day 1970, a date that represents both a national awakening on this topic and my own first exposure to it as a junior in high school. Scientists have shown us how serious our problems are, and they are coming up with solutions. In fact, I've been surprised by the cautious optimism now being expressed by some prominent voices, such as E. O. Wilson of Harvard. He believes that it is possible for the human race to navigate through the worst of the crisis in the next fifty or seventy-five years—not easily, mind you, but possible.

Scientists can only do so much, however. From our human perspective, the future of God's creation—and the human race—is in the hands of politicians, lawyers and teachers, businessmen and women, engineers and architects. Present and future pastors, teachers and ordinary Christians in particular hold the fate of creation in their hands. By the end of my tenure at Au Sable Institute, I had become convinced that the whole church of Jesus Christ, and the ordinary people who are its members, are the best and perhaps the only hope for a true solution to the global environmental crisis.

What about God? Where is he in all of this? We sing and we believe that "his eye is on the sparrow"—surely the future of his creation is in his hands, not ours? God would not allow us to destroy his creation, would he?

Well, yes. He might. It is absolutely true that God is in sovereign control of history: "I make known the end from the beginning," he says. "My purpose will stand, and I will do all that I please" (Isaiah 46:10). That is a biblical given. However, within the framework of God's plan for history, he has and does allow us human beings an astonishing amount of latitude in what we do with our lives, our surroundings—and yes, what we do with and to his creation. It is abundantly clear from history, ancient and modern, that God allows holocausts and wars and all kinds of terrible things to take place. There is no objective reason—and certainly no biblical one—for saying that God would step in to prevent us as a race from causing the planet he gave us to become unlivable. He has allowed us to build weapons that could erase life on the planet in a matter of minutes. If we choose to destroy our home, God will not stop us.

Unless, that is, God were to step into history the way he usually does, through human beings who have aligned their lives with him and who are committed to accomplishing his purposes in their own small histories. Remember God's invitation to Moses in Exodus? God said, "I have indeed seen the misery of my people in Egypt. I have heard them crying out . . . and I am concerned about their suffering. So I have come down to rescue them" (3:7-8). And then the clincher: "So now, go. I am sending *you* to Pharaoh to bring my people the Israelites out of Egypt" (v. 10, emphasis added). When God wants to do something in the world, he does step in, but he does it through people.

I believe God has seen the sufferings of human beings around the world (see chapter one for a brief survey of the pain the environmental crisis is causing), and I believe he is ready to step in to reverse the ecological disaster we have brought on ourselves. And he is calling his church to take up this task on his behalf: "So now, go. I am sending *you*."

God has recruited some unusual prophets to the cause. Consider E. O. Wilson's recent book, *The Creation*. Wilson is a confirmed religious skeptic and secularist, but he has written an appeal to a fictional Southern Baptist pastor, asking for his help:

> You and I and every other human being strive for the same imperatives of security, freedom of choice, personal dignity, and a cause to believe in that is larger than ourselves. Let us see, then, if we can, and you are willing, to meet on the near side of metaphysics in order to deal with the real world we share. I put it this way because *you have the power to help solve a great problem about which I care deeply. I hope you have the same concern. I suggest that we set aside our differences in order to save the Creation. . . . Pastor, we need your help. The Creation— living Nature—is in deep trouble.*[1]

In much of his book, Wilson could have phrased his appeal a bit more tactfully. He makes clear the many ways in which he expects that he and his pastoral colleague disagree and why his rational, scientific, secular position is superior to what he presumes the pastor believes. But still, he is asking for help.

All of this is a remarkable reversal from 1967, when Lynn White laid the blame for our modern environmental crisis at the feet of Christianity in his essay "The Historical Roots of our Ecologic Crisis":

> Modern technology is at least partly to be explained as an Occidental and voluntarist realizing of the Christian dogma of man's transcendence of, and rightful mastery over, nature. But, as we now recognize, somewhat over a century ago science and tech-

nology—hitherto quite separate activities—joined to give man-
kind powers which, to judge by man of the ecologic effects, are
out of control. *If so, Christianity bears a huge burden of guilt.*[2]

This is not so, as numbers of writers have demonstrated in the
years since. Many of White's readers did not realize that he himself
concluded his essay with an implicit recognition that, whatever the
source of the problem, religion has to be part of the solution:

> Since *the roots of our trouble are so largely religious, the remedy
> must also be essentially religious,* whether we call it that or not. We
> must rethink and refeel our nature and destiny. The profoundly
> religious, but heretical, sense of the primitive Franciscans for the
> spiritual autonomy of all parts of nature may point a direction. I
> propose Francis as a patron saint for ecologists.[3]

And now we have Wilson recognizing that "religion and science
are the two most powerful forces in the world today."[4] He has in
mind the power of influence—both popular and political. Evangelical Christians are reckoned as a powerful political force, and their
possibility of popular influence is obvious. There are millions of
people in church every Sunday. If religious leaders, or just evangelical leaders, were to speak with a single voice, people would listen.
In this, Wilson is right: it would be no small thing if the thirty million evangelicals in the United States and many more around the
world were recruited into a global effort to reverse the damage now
being done to our world.

But the ability to influence people is not the only or even the best
role the church can play. My convictions about the role of the church
in this crisis come from a belief that environmental problems are sin
problems. There is an underlying spiritual dissonance in the universe
that makes it impossible for us to live within our means and in harmony with the natural systems that support our lives. We are out of
touch with the One who runs the place. Therefore the most careful
science and the best economic theories and the most profound gov-

ernmental policies will never be enough. *We have a spiritual problem, and we need a spiritual solution.*

Solving spiritual problems is what the church is all about, and that's what we can bring to the table in this crisis. We call it redemption—God's plan and provision to reconcile all things to himself—and it applies as much to our environmental crisis as it does to every other aspect of our lives. That this is not immediately evident in the current actions of the church will be no surprise to you. We in the church have been moderately energetic in seeking to respond to many needs that we see in the world. We feed the hungry and we heal the sick. I have spent time personally in disaster response efforts, and I've seen that the most effective agencies for disaster relief are often Christian organizations. When we see and understand a need, we respond enthusiastically, generously and usually effectively. But not when it comes to environmental issues.

My experience has been like that of many others in this field. Simple conversations often reveal a serious disconnect between my view of the environmental crisis and that of many other evangelical Christians. During one business trip, I was visiting a local church. A member welcomed me before the service began, asking me what brought me to their town. "I work with a Christian environmental organization," I replied—and there was a long, long pause.

"A what?" he asked.

I repeated myself.

Another silence, then he replied, "I didn't know there was such a thing." He not only didn't know it, but the question in his eyes told me he wasn't too sure it was possible or that it would be a very good idea. I wondered later if the particularly enthusiastic altar call at the end of the service was for me.

At Urbana 03, InterVarsity's triennial student missions convention, I participated as an exhibitor on behalf of Au Sable Institute. I found myself besieged by students throughout the conference. Au Sable was the only organization among hundreds present that had "environment" anywhere in its name or ministry description, and only a handful of others had anything to offer students concerned with this issue.

Three years later, at Urbana 06, I represented a new organization, Care of Creation, Inc., in the same capacity and led a seminar on missions and the environment. The seminar was packed with more than four hundred students, primarily because it was the only scheduled event in the five-day conference that touched on environmental issues. Students could not believe this. They were environmental studies majors, environmental science majors or in many cases just students who were aware of the environmental crisis and saw it as one of the great needs of the day. They wanted to serve the kingdom of God by working to address the abuse of God's creation that they could see all around them. They could not understand why this problem, so apparent to them, seemed not even to exist in the world of Christian missions organizations.

This was what led Craig Sorley to write to me from Kenya. He wanted to "do environmental missions" the way many organizations "do medical missions." Where traditional medical missions seek to heal people through clinics, hospitals and public health programs while sharing the good news of Jesus, Craig would "heal the earth" through tree planting and similar projects, while sharing the news of the gospel. But it appeared he needed a new kind of missions organization.

Susanna and I prayed much about this opportunity. Finally, knowing the risks but believing God was guiding us, we decided to accept Craig's invitation. He and I worked together on a proposal for such an organization for the next few months and sought the advice of many friends and acquaintances. The result was the birth of Care of Creation, Inc., in April 2005.

Our vision statement captures the goal we each had in mind when we began:

Mobilizing the worldwide church toward
a God-centered response to the environmental crisis
that brings glory to the Creator,

advances the cause of Christ
and leads to a transformation of the people
and the land that sustains them.

You will notice that three-fourths of our mission statement has to do
with God: we are looking for a "God-centered" response that brings
him glory and that advances the "cause of Christ." These are theological concepts that we are applying to very real and messy problems. The
challenges presented by the environmental crisis exist: people are suffering. Solutions will require us to get our hands dirty. We don't believe
that Bible study can take the place of planting trees or that theological
propositions will end soil erosion. But we do believe that an approach
to the environmental crisis that is theologically sound, scientifically informed and implemented by a community of redeemed people acting
out of love for God and for each other—that is what the church is, after
all—can do what no one else has been able to do.

Care of Creation is off to a strong start. Craig's project in Kenya is
in the process of encouraging churches and schools in many parts of
the country to teach biblically based creation care and to develop their
own tree nurseries to provide seedlings for their people to plant. We're
working to establish the week after Easter every year as a National
Tree Planting week in celebration of the resurrection. And we're embarking on plans to extend our work throughout East Africa as per-
sonnel and funds become available.

We are excited about the work God has given us, but we're only one
small organization trying to make an impact in one corner of God's
wonderful world. This book is not about our organization; it is about
the whole church, God's people everywhere, waking up to the problems
and opportunities represented by the environmental crisis we see in the
world today. The problems we are seeing in Kenya are repeated in
Southeast Asia and Latin America, in China and India. And the church
is present in all these places. But we also see great possibilities if the
church in the United States, Canada and other "developed" countries
were to mobilize, for much of the damage to the globe originates in

these countries, even though the effects are being felt far away.

At Care of Creation we use the term *mobilization* by design. It carries a certain military aspect that conveys urgency. It also suggests a deployment of resources that already exist, and that is an important part of my thesis. The church needs to change little to be effective in the environmental crisis. We have the beliefs; we have the people; we have programs in place. We don't need to invent anything—we simply need to go to work. Open the warehouse doors and move out the equipment!

By this point it should be obvious that I come from an evangelical background. My experiences, stories and, I suspect, even my language reflect that origin, and I am naturally thinking of my fellow evangelicals as I write. This is not meant to exclude anyone. Whatever your church (or nonchurch) background might be, I hope you'll come with me along this brief journey, and maybe through it you will understand the heart of evangelical Christianity a bit better. You are most welcome!

A word on the structure of the book: In chapter one I'll outline the current environmental crisis in broad strokes. Please keep in mind that this survey is not intended to be exhaustive; if you want to dig more deeply into any aspect of our current crisis, please take a look at some of the resources listed in appendix four. Our crisis today is different from what we faced in 1970 and much more frightening. Water, deforestation, soil erosion, pollution—the gauges that measure a host of problems are rapidly climbing from "danger" to "critical," and this without even bringing climate change into the picture.

I will not spend much time discussing climate change. This is a significant part of the crisis we're facing today, but it's not the only environmental crisis looming over us. Some may be hoping that the climate-change prognosticators are wrong, and that if they are, we can relax and carry on with business as usual. *Nothing could be further from the truth.* Even if the (apparently overwhelming) evidence for human-induced climate change turns out to be wrong, God's creation is still in deep trouble. In fact, many of the things I personally am worried about—such as the availability of fresh water—will reach a critical stage long before we feel the serious effects of climate change.

Chapters two through six are an examination of biblical truths—doctrines—that point us to an active and robust caring for God's creation. The church is a theological organization; in nonreligious language, we could say that it is values-based. We are going to find that the theology broadly accepted among evangelicals contains a ready-made foundation for a response to the environmental crisis. These chapters are a discussion of a few of the major doctrines that are important in this regard: creation, incarnation, sin, redemption and the church. Other doctrines could have been included, but these, to me, form a solid and powerful argument that the church can—and must—respond to the environmental crisis by actively caring for God's creation.

Chapters seven through twelve discuss the mobilization of the church in practical terms, from worship and education to facilities and missions programs. Remember the term *mobilization*. We want to activate resources that are already in place. Much of what's needed is already present in almost every congregation or church fellowship. Your own church has a variety of activities and programs now underway that can be powerful instruments in response to the environmental crisis. Adding creation care need not displace existing programs. Think of it rather as a "mix-in" (as in one of those gourmet ice cream shops) that will enrich every aspect of church life it touches—and save scarce ministry dollars as well. There is no need for a church to feel more stretched because it chose to emphasize creation care throughout its range of ministry activities; in almost every case, good environmental stewardship will mean good financial stewardship as well.

The final chapter is a brief appeal to the people who will be key in the mobilization of the church: pastors, ordinary church members and particularly students. If the whole church is to mobilize, it will only happen if many individual churches become concerned and active—and this will happen only if individual people decide that this is important enough to do something about. For in the end, a church is what its members are, and a church does what its members decide to do.

PART 1

The Message
Why the Church Must Care for Creation

1

Running on Empty

Things are not always as they appear.

As I write these words, it's a glorious day in southern Wisconsin. I live in an "inner suburb" of Madison, a medium-size city. I'm surrounded by about two hundred thousand other human beings, but there's little evidence of an environmental crisis in what I see today. "God's in his heaven, all's right with the world" would sum things up quite nicely. The sky is blue, with white puffy clouds. The air is just a bit chill, with the promise of frost in a couple of weeks. Bright yellow leaves on some of the trees stand out against the dark green of some of their fellows, who have not yet felt the coming of winter. High overhead an occasional V of geese meanders toward the south. Environmental crisis? What crisis?

If you were to join me in the dining room of my house, we could look out over the back deck, across a small cul-de-sac, and see a lovely prairie, perhaps two hundred yards from my house. It's home to a variety of birds, small mammals and many creatures I've never met. To our left, behind a tall clump of trees, is a small pond that hosts ducks and geese, and probably a few fish, though no neighborhood child has to my knowledge ever succeeded in catching any. A bike trail winds past the prairie and around the pond, connecting with one of the best city bike trail systems in the country. I could ride nine miles to the center of the city and spend only one mile of that distance on city streets. Or I could walk a block and catch a city bus that would take me to the same place in about the same amount of time. It would appear that I am living in a perfect example of a modern urban/suburban development that has kept in touch with nature. There are people everywhere, but there are still trees, green grass and even this beautiful prairie.

What you don't know is that the prairie covers a former city dump. An innocent-looking utility building to the right, just out of sight from our deck vantage point, is a sophisticated methane recovery system that runs night and day. It was installed after a house just like mine exploded a number of years ago. Neighbors still talk about it. Apparently methane from the dump infiltrated the basement and found its way to the furnace or water-heater pilot light. The resulting explosion was spectacular. Even now, if you purchase a house bordering the "prairie," you will inherit a thick set of documents advising you that, while the city is doing its best to protect you by collecting methane from the unseen waste, there are no guarantees that your house will not explode like the first one did.

An Invisible Crisis

A restored prairie that hides a dangerous landfill is a picture of the environmental crisis we face today. In April 1970, we celebrated the very first Earth Day. I was a junior in high school, and I found myself somewhat unwillingly participating in the festivities in the industrial town of Fitchburg, Massachusetts. My homeroom teacher had drafted me to deliver one of the "talks" on the environmental crisis. His name, his face and my speech are lost to history, but the event is not. Earth Day could not have come too soon for Fitchburg.

Our city was a paper-manufacturing center. The local mills had been long accustomed to using the Nashua River, running through the center of town, as a convenient outlet for their waste. We teenagers were proud of the fact that the river changed color by the day, depending on what color the current batch of paper was. I have no recollection as to what I actually said at that school assembly thirty some years ago, but I'm very much aware of the difference Earth Day has made in Fitchburg, and in the entire country.

Thanks to that first Earth Day, and the attention paid to it by Congress, a raft of legislation was passed requiring clean air, clean water and protection for species in danger of going out of existence. Evidence for the success of that effort is abundant everywhere; not long ago, the bald eagle was declared no longer at risk of extinction and was removed from the Endangered Species list. Even Fitchburg has changed. Today you could swim in the Nashua River. Knowing what I know of its history, I wouldn't recommend it—but still, you could.

We took care of the colored rivers. Most of us still live in the midst of green grass, and birds come to our backyard feeders. On most days, for most of us, the air is breathable. So, mostly, things don't look so bad. It might be possible to believe that we solved the environmental crisis with the actions begun in 1970, just as it might be possible to believe that a restored prairie is simply a benign, grass-and-flower-covered hillside. Until a house blows up. It might be helpful to remember that you can't see the methane until it explodes. Then it's too late.

Yes, we still have a crisis. In some parts of the world, it's all too visible, as if the dump behind my house had never been covered at all. And the results are often tragic for the people who live there. In late September 2004 Hurricane Jeanne, the fifth major storm of that year's hurricane season, ravaged the Caribbean and eastern United States. Millions of people were affected, and the storm caused substantial damage everywhere. But the casualty figures are stunning: Jeanne killed five people in the continental United States, seven in Puerto Rico, eighteen in the Dominican Republic, but more than three thousand in Haiti. Why? More than other countries affected, Haiti had suffered catastrophic environmental damage before the storm. Less than 1 percent of Haiti's forest was intact, and without trees to hold back soil and absorb rainfall, even modest showers can turn into mudslides. Jeanne's thirteen inches of rain on the mountains above the city of Gonaives caused an avalanche of mud that affected eighty thousand people.

But even in North America, problems like my hidden city dump still exist. You can't see that underground water levels are dropping, but they are—between thirty and three hundred feet per year in North

America and around the world, from Kansas and Nebraska to China and India. The green lawns and beautiful golf courses we take as a sign of health and beauty are a product of chemical poisons that contribute to the destruction of vast numbers of creatures. Even our blankets and frying pans are the source of hundreds of man-made chemicals in our bloodstreams.

E. O. Wilson sums up the situation thus:

> Humanity is already the first species in the history of life to become a geophysical force. We have, all by our bipedal, wobbly headed selves, altered Earth's atmosphere and climate away from the norm. We have spread thousands of toxic chemicals worldwide, appropriated 40% of the solar energy available for photosynthesis, converted almost all of the easily arable land, dammed most of the rivers, raised the planet sea level, and now, in a manner likely to get everyone's attention like nothing else before it, we are close to running out of fresh water. A collateral of all of this frenetic activity is the continuing extinction of wild ecosystems, along with the species that compose them. This happens to be the only human impact that is irreversible.[1]

A Different Kind of Crisis

Today's crisis is qualitatively different from that which we faced thirty-five years ago. The problems then, though widespread, were essentially local in nature. One river or watershed was contaminated and could be fixed. One city had substandard air quality, and regulations could be imposed. What is clear now is that *the crisis we face is global.* It is worldwide in extent, and interconnected systems that we do not understand are being impacted. Globalization is not new; God's biosphere has always functioned globally. All parts are connected, and human impact has increased to the point that the entire system is under threat. Every local problem is caused by or causes problems in other corners of the world. Loss of rainforest cover in the Amazon affects climate in North America and Europe. Toxic air pollution in

China descends in the rain of California and Oregon. Chemicals pumped into the atmosphere around the world show up in the blood and breast milk of people living above the Arctic Circle.

But even yesterday's local problems turn out to have global complications. In 1970, the concern of the citizens of Fitchburg, Massachusetts, was for the health of the Nashua River. It was a local problem. The cause was nearby. The solution seemed easy: reroute or treat the industrial waste. In fact, most of the paper mills closed. Paper is still being produced, and rivers are still changing color, but now the rivers are in China or Indonesia. Moving the problem from one city to another, from one watershed to another, doesn't make it go away.

It is a big problem, and it is complicated. We can only scratch the surface here. Rather than getting overwhelmed with details that others have examined exhaustively, I'd like to discuss some patterns that seem to emerge from the data, patterns that show why today's crisis is different from any we have experienced before.

People, People Everywhere

It is a population crisis. The United States recently welcomed its 300-millionth resident with much media fanfare. No one was sure if the newcomer was an infant born somewhere in Middle America or an immigrant at Kennedy airport with two suitcases and a work permit. But it's instructive to note that Atlanta attorney Bobby Woo, whom *Life* magazine designated the 200-millionth American when he was born in November 1967, was only thirty-nine years old when number 300 million came along. In his lifetime, world population has approximately doubled, from three billion to six billion people. Quite simply, there are more people alive on earth now than ever before. In fact, there may be more people alive on earth now *than have ever lived in all of human history.*

This simple fact—that we as human beings have multiplied beyond expectation—overshadows every other challenge raised by the environmental crisis. Increasing population forces the expansion of urban areas and the consequent loss of habitat for large segments of God's (nonhuman) creation. It strains everything from transportation networks to health systems. Every potential advance in environmental stewardship falls to the relentless pressure of increased numbers of people. We might be able to develop an automobile that is 50 percent more efficient than today's models—in fact, we can—but if we double the number of cars on the road, we'll still be 50 percent behind. At the other end of the technological spectrum, in those parts of the world where human life still depends on growing one's own food on small plots of land, the effect of large families can be seen directly. A plot that fed five people a generation ago now has to feed forty. Even if we were able to double or triple the productivity of the land—instead of watching it decline by those factors, as is actually happening in many places—the present generation would still have less to eat than their parents did.

We who are Christians are troubled by this because we place a high value on human life. Every person is precious in God's sight; all are created in his image. We would go further: every human being should be able to live and eat and love and worship. Every human being created by God deserves the opportunity to know and love his Creator. The Bible applied universal dignity and meaning to the life of every human being long before the American Declaration of Independence enshrined the concept of inalienable rights. We rightly abhor government policies such as forced abortion and forced sterilization. But this means we face a dilemma: how can we confront the problems raised by increasing numbers of precious people and still recognize and honor each one's uniqueness and dignity?

Some suggest that our increased population doesn't have to be a problem. For example, Japan appears to have managed a high population density, a high standard of living and good environmental quality all at the same time. If all countries were like Japan, population would not be a problem.

Well, not exactly. No one can reasonably predict an entire globe with the population density of Japan and the same high economic and environmental standards. It's not going to happen. Here's why: Japan has strong governmental leadership, an economic base that can support technological solutions and, probably, the people of Japan are motivated by the obvious limitations imposed by the fact that their homeland is an island. Managing a large, high-density population requires a disciplined society and an efficient, responsive and incorrupt government, and Japan has these. All these factors contribute to its environmental success, making it a significant exception among nations.

In 1948 Frank Gilbreth Jr. and his sister Ernestine Gilbreth Carey wrote *Cheaper By the Dozen* about their experiences growing up in a household of twelve children. The family's survival—and the source of much hilarity in the story—was due to Dad's rigorous application of the new field of industrial efficiency techniques to family life:

> Dad installed process and work charts in the bathrooms. Every child old enough to write—and Dad expected his offspring to start writing at a tender age—was required to initial the charts in the morning after he had brushed his teeth, taken a bath, combed his hair, and made his bed. At night, each child had to weigh himself, plot the figure on a graph, and initial the process charts again after he had done his homework, washed his hands and face and brushed his teeth. Mother wanted to have a place on the charts for saying prayers, but Dad said as far as he was concerned prayers were voluntary.
>
> It was regimentation, all right. But bear in mind the trouble most parents have in getting just one child off to school, and multiply it by twelve. *Some regimentation was necessary to prevent bedlam.*[2]

A family of twelve children was able to run smoothly, and still love each other, because of tight discipline and careful management. It's the same way with countries. True, Japan has done it, but discipline and careful management are in short supply in most countries where population is a serious problem.

The Japanese experience is also misleading because Japan has kept itself clean by shifting the dirt to its neighbors. In some ways it paral-

lels my story about Fitchburg. Fitchburg cleaned its river by exporting
the pollution to other places when the local paper mills closed and re-
opened elsewhere. Japan has done the same thing. For example, it has
maintained extensive forests at home, but is one of the major sources
of tropical deforestation in Indonesia. Japan's appetite for ocean sea-
food is voracious, and ocean fisheries far from her coasts are showing
the strain. It would not be able to maintain its environmental or economic standards without importing resources from—and thereby exporting the accompanying problems to—other countries.

Even the "good news" about population can be problematic. In
many areas of the world, population growth has stopped, and in some
places it is actually declining. Recent figures show that as many as sixteen countries have stable or declining populations, with fertility rates
below 2.1 per woman, which is the accepted number of births necessary to maintain a population at a constant level. These include
Ukraine, with a fertility rate of 1.1 births per woman; Russia, 1.2;
Spain, 1.3; Japan, Germany, Italy and Romania, 1.3; and so on. Even
China makes this list now, with a fertility rate of 1.8. There is a general
consensus that by about 2050 the total human population will level
out at between 8 and 10 billion people and, based on the experience
of countries already past their peak population growth periods, will
probably begin a slow decline. Harsh government policies are not going to be responsible for this; in fact, they have seldom worked well.
The projected leveling off and gradual decline will be the result of
what has happened all over the world as education of women and effective medical care have become available.[3]

Now, why should this be a problem? If an ever-increasing population is a problem, wouldn't a stable or slowly decreasing population
be a blessing? Environmentally, yes. Economically, no. The shift from
increasing to stable to declining populations is going to send shock-
waves through the world's economies. Our economic systems are
built on the basis of ever-increasing numbers of people producing
and consuming ever-increasing amounts of goods, services and
money. Pension systems in particular are predicated on the assump-

tion that there will be an increasing supply of younger workers to pay for and care for those who have retired. When populations mature—as in many European countries and soon in the United States as well—these systems are finding themselves in great difficulty. We can't go on growing indefinitely—that's clear. But our current economic system means that we can't be prosperous *without* growing indefinitely. One of baseball's most interesting plays develops when a runner is caught between bases with opponents on either side of him. It's called a pickle, and it almost always results in the runner being tagged out. It looks like the human race is caught in a historical pickle such as we've never seen before.

There's a more immediate problem, though—that of population distribution. While sixteen countries have stable fertility rates, many more do not. The Earth Policy Institute listed thirty-three countries with fertility rates ranging from 2.3 (Vietnam) to 7.0 (Democratic Republic of Congo) in 2002.[4] So even while some countries begin the process of population decline, others are still expanding rapidly.

You would think there would be an easy solution here, even if it only bought some time: encourage people living in countries still growing rapidly to move to those countries facing a shortage of younger workers. This would even out the environmental burden and alleviate economic difficulties caused by a lack of workers, giving all of us time to work out longer-term solutions. Unfortunately, it is by no means clear that such people will be able to move or that they will be welcome when they arrive. Anti-immigration initiatives throughout the developed world would tend to suggest that the "solution" of redistributing population is not going to be easy.

A friend of mine has a small summer cottage in northern Michigan. Through unfortunate planning when the house was built, it has an undersized septic tank situated close to a neighboring pond. When there aren't many people staying at the house, the system can keep up with the demands placed on it—that is, it can handle perhaps two showers and five or six toilet flushes in a twenty-four-hour period. Anything more than that, watch out! When more than two people are using the toilet and taking showers, the tank fills and backs up into the house, causing more than a little inconvenience. The world's population situation is like my friend's septic tank problem. His house could have beds for five, ten or fifteen people, but that doesn't matter. If the plumbing can't handle all those people, there's no point trying to fill all the beds. If by some measures many more people could fit on the earth, by other, more fundamental measures the system is already overloaded. The plumbing is backing up.

This backup happens in two opposite but equally problematic ways: some of us have too much of a good thing while many others don't have enough of anything.

Too Much of a Good Thing

The environmental crisis is thus more than a population crisis. *It is a prosperity crisis.* We are witnessing a remarkable and unprecedented transformation of economics, business and culture in the world today. Tom Friedman, *New York Times* columnist and author of *The World Is Flat* and *The Lexus and the Olive Tree,* has watched and analyzed as well as anyone what is now known as globalization:

> The force that gives [globalization] its unique character—is the newfound power for individuals to collaborate and compete globally. . . . The flat-world platform is the product of a convergence of the personal computer (which allowed every individual to suddenly become the author of his or her own content in digital form) with fiber optic cable (which suddenly allowed all those individuals to access more and more digital content around the world for next to nothing) with the rise of work flow software (which enabled individuals all over the world to collaborate on that same digital content from anywhere, regardless of the distances between them). No one anticipated this convergence. It just happened—right around the year 2000.[5]

Globalization has been controversial. Many have benefited; many have been hurt. But no one questions that it is real and it is here. And it's hard to avoid the conclusion that globalization has generated more material wealth for more people in a shorter length of time than ever before in history. Globalization has not eliminated global poverty, but it *has* brought the possibility of a Western-style, consumer-oriented lifestyle within the reach of millions of people around the world. And there is where we find the problem.

A unified global economy that brings prosperity to millions who have been previously left out could sink the entire global ship—or, to switch metaphors, bring down the global airliner. Not long ago I accepted a seven-month assignment to work on a response to the Pakistan earthquake of 2005. I found myself traveling a great deal. Because I was alone I was able to travel light, usually with just one suitcase. This was not true of many of my fellow passengers. Every time I checked in, I watched as one or another unfortunate family learned that they could not bring all the suitcases they wanted to. The cases were too heavy, or there were too many of them, or (often) both. I sympathized with them—I've been there myself at times—but I also understood why the airlines have limitations on baggage. If everyone brings everything they want, the plane will never get off the ground. This in fact happened on one of the flights I was to take. I saw a mountain of luggage to one side of the baggage hall and learned that the previous flight had been overweight and all of this baggage had been removed and would have to go on another flight.

Weight limits are written into the laws of the physical universe. They determine that a line has to be drawn, or the results will be catastrophic. Our global economy is like one of those planes. Until recently, we've had a few passengers who've been traveling with twenty or thirty suitcases each—primarily those of us living in North America and Europe. We could do this because most of the passengers in the rear of the plane haven't had any luggage at all. The unlooked-for arrival of globalization means more and more of these passengers are able to bring five, seven or ten suitcases of their own. The result is easily predictable: the capacity of this plane is rapidly running out.

The World Wildlife Fund recently released its 2006 "Living Planet

Report" estimating that the human race as a whole was exceeding the sustainable capacity of the earth by 25 percent in 2003, the most recent year for which statistics were available. Estimates were that we would raise this to an overdraft of 30 percent in 2006, and this would increase to 100 percent by 2050. Consider the consumption rates anticipated for just one country, China.[6] According to author Lester Brown, if the Chinese economy continues to expand at current rates, and if Chinese consumers attain levels of personal consumption similar to those in the United States, both of which are easy to foresee, in twenty-five years China will need

- two-thirds of the world's entire current grain harvest;
- double the world's current manufacturing capacity of paper;
- 99 million barrels of oil per day (total global production is now "only" 84 million barrels per day)[7]

Obviously such a situation is not possible. The globe cannot produce enough paper to double the portion China uses and still allow for the rest of the world's use. Same with oil. Grain. Steel. Bottom line: the world cannot support an entire globe of people living at the standard Americans and Europeans take for granted. But they're trying to—and will continue to do so until we all agree on how much we each can bring on board.

Not Enough of Anything

Paradoxically, *the global environmental crisis is also a poverty crisis*. For every new consumer seeking to benefit from the prosperity of globalization, there are hundreds doomed to lives of utter misery. Dickens's line "it was the best of times, it was the worst of times" may never have been as starkly true as it is today. In too many countries, too many people are trying to eke a living out of plots of land that are simply too small and too depleted to support human beings any longer.

The staff of my organization, Care of Creation, reported recently from a meeting with several farmers in the small village of Tiekunu, Kenya, near the edge of the Rift Valley. These farmers have been cultivating the same family plots for more than thirty years. We asked them what typical harvests were like in 1975, compared with 2006. This is what we learned:

- Corn production in 1975 was 30 bags[8] per acre; today, 7 bags per acre.
- Bean production in 1975, 20 bags per acre; today, 5 bags per acre.
- Potato production in 1975, 100 bags per acre; today, 10 bags per acre.

This is in an area where increased population means more people need to live off the same plots of land—in some cases, many more people. Such agricultural statistics indicate both the result of environmental damage to the soil and a certain prediction of more to come, as poverty-stricken families force the land to try to produce more and more with less and less. While the wealthy in the front of the plane threaten it by loading on more and more suitcases, the poor at the back scrape the very insulation off the wires in an attempt to survive.

The challenges are not simply due to attempts to squeeze more people onto ancient family farms, however. The arrival of globalization does bring prosperity, but often it brings environmental disaster as well. This is the dark side of globalization. Large corporations can easily move their businesses anywhere they wish around the world. Sometimes they are looking for lower wages; in other cases, the corporate ideal is little or no environmental regulation. The result is that prosperous consumers of North America and Europe are able to keep their local environments clean by exporting the toxic effects of modern manufacturing to other communities in desperate need of jobs. A country trying to limit environmental damage often faces the prospect of losing the factories they seek to regulate, as multinationals simply move the work to a less assertive or more corrupt country.

Rural China is an example, though people in every other "less developed" country are in the same situation. We see frequent news from China, reporting toxic spills in major rivers affecting millions of people, including one in 2005 that may have involved more than one

hundred tons of benzene, an industrial solvent, released into the Son-
ghua River. What may be even more tragic are reports now coming out
of other areas in rural China where chronic pollution is causing massive increases in cancer and other environmentally triggered diseases,
some of which are caused by toxic metals from electronic components
shipped from the United States and Europe for recycling.

China's food industry is reeling from scandal after scandal involv-
ing the substitution of industrial ingredients in food and pharmaceu-
tical products that have been exported around the world, including to
Ecuador, where children have died from contaminated acetami-
nophen syrup, and to the United States, where pets have suffered kid-
ney failure and other problems from contaminated pet food.

Of course, the environmental price paid by the poor is evident in
the United States as well. Maybe you wondered why I live adjacent to
a landfill that could blow up my house or the one next to mine.[9] It
happens that this is a house I can afford. I'm not by any means among
the poorest in Madison, but many of my neighbors are. Houses here
are nice, small and cheap; we make up the price difference in the environmental risk we assume from the landfill next door. You won't
find many hybrid vehicles on this street; the vehicle of choice is an old
minivan or wheezing Chevrolet Caprice or Ford Taurus. Some of us
have good, tight insulation for our homes, but most of the rental prop-
erties here lack even storm doors to keep heat in during the bitter Wisconsin winters. My neighborhood endures more environmental risk
and does more damage to God's creation in the process of living than
those who live in more affluent neighborhoods just a few streets away,
who can afford energy-efficient cars and appliances, and might even
be able to install solar panels on their houses.

A "Perfect Storm"

Inevitably, the "perfect storm" of population, prosperity and poverty
is resulting in a *global political crisis*. Politics is the way we human beings manage our public affairs. It's how we decide everything, and it
would be foolish not to expect that an environmental crisis of such

proportions would spill over into the political realm. We should worry about political threats arising from specific environmental problems. Water wars in the Middle East are a real menace in that region beset by so many other tensions. However, our bigger concern should be the overall level of stress that environmentally devastated countries experience, creating internal tensions that often cause or contribute to international disputes and even international terrorism.

A list of the countries experiencing environmental stress (Afghanistan, Haiti, Indonesia, Nepal, Pakistan, Rwanda and Somalia, to name just a few) would be almost identical to a list of those experiencing the greatest political tensions internally and externally. Political tensions in these regions may be one more way environmental problems are making themselves known and crying out to be resolved. The question, according to author Jared Diamond, is whether we will solve them ourselves, rationally, or allow them to solve themselves. One way or another, they will be resolved.

> The only question is whether they will become resolved in pleasant ways of our own choice, or in unpleasant ways not of our choice, such as warfare, genocide, starvation, disease epidemics, and collapses of societies. While all of those grim phenomena have been endemic to humanity throughout our history, *their frequency increases with environmental degradation, population pressure, and the resulting poverty and instability. . . .*
>
> When people are desperate, undernourished, and without hope, they blame their governments, which they see as responsible for or unable to solve their problems. They try to emigrate at any cost. They fight each other over land. They kill each other. They start civil wars. They figure they have nothing to lose, so they become terrorists, or they support or tolerate terrorism.[10]

Surely it is better to resolve problems "in pleasant ways of our own choice" rather than to allow these things to resolve themselves. But what does that mean? It means discussion, cooperation and compromise. It means looking beyond and behind the symptoms that present themselves, in order to find underlying causes. It means having the imagination to come up with original solutions for unprecedented problems and the courage to propose and carry out those solutions.

But if that is all this crisis requires, we should be on our way to recovery. In the last four or five years there has been a worldwide explosion of ideas. Hybrid cars. Buildings that produce energy instead of consuming it. Farming techniques that produce more food on less and leave the soil more fertile than before. Imagination is *not* our problem. We know how to do what needs to be done.

So why do we still have a problem? That is what we need to figure out. And to do that, we have to go back to the very beginning. We have to start with God.

2

By Him and for Him

As I sit at my desk, I can see a set of three handmade mugs. They aren't high art, but they're attractive and functional. They could sell for a decent price in the kind of store that sells hand-made pottery.

But these mugs aren't for sale. And I don't think I'll be using them very often, if at all. Why? Because I know who made them. I have a special relationship with her, and these mugs remind me of her, especially now that she's no longer a daily part of my life. She's my youngest daughter. I could show you, in various corners of my house, all kinds of other things that one or another of my four children has made. In the kitchen is the most unusual set of salt and pepper shakers you've ever seen, and in boxes in the basement lie treasure troves of school papers and awards. These are all commercially worthless and pretty much useless to anyone outside our family. But my wife and I keep them. Why? These things—mugs, papers, drawings, award certificates—take their worth from the relationships that surround them. I value them because I value the people who made them.

My biggest reason for caring for God's creation has nothing to do with the extent or the severity of the crisis, the number of people affected or even the ultimate future of the human race. It has to do with one simple fact: I know the God who made it all. And I love him. If I can place a high price on things that have little or no intrinsic value simply because they were made by one of my children, how much more ought I to value and care for this amazing world God made, this world that is precious because he made it and that represents an excellence and beauty far beyond anything that any of us could begin to comprehend, let alone make on our own.

"Who" Matters

The first verses of Genesis tell us that God made the world, but they don't tell us much else. We don't know how, we don't know when, we don't really hear why. We actually get a better handle on God's creative process from Paul's letter to the Colossians:

> [Jesus Christ] is the image of the invisible God, the firstborn over all creation. *For by him all things were created:* things in heaven and on earth, visible and invisible, whether thrones or powers or rulers or authorities; *all things were created by him and for him.* He is before all things, and *in him all things hold together.* (1:15-17, emphasis added)

If you're like me, when you think about God creating, you think about God the Father. However, Paul is quite clear here that the agent of creation was Jesus Christ—the person who came, lived among us, died and rose from the dead—the One who saved us from our sins. Certainly the other members of the Trinity are present at creation, as Genesis 1:26 would seem to suggest ("let us make man in our image"), but Paul seems to suggest that Christ's role in creation is preeminent: he is the Creator: "by him all things were created." He is the sustainer: "in him all things hold together." And perhaps most important, he is the reason for it all: "all things were created . . . for him." I'm sure you've seen the Christmastime bumper sticker: "Jesus is the Reason for the Season." Yes, and he's the reason for the trees. For the butterflies. For the fish in the sea and the clouds in the sky. The reason you and I exist.

And this Person, whom John called *Logos* (Greek for "the Word"; see John 1:1), is the One I call my Savior. The relationship here is much closer than my relationship with the maker of the mugs on my desk. If I call myself a Christian or a Christ-follower, I'm following the One who made everything. The One for whom everything was made. The One who holds all the molecules in everything together. *Everything* means me. And you. Your family members. The neighbor across the street. My dog. Your cat and your parakeets and the rabbits and squirrels in the yard. The dandelions and creeping Charlie that decorate my lawn. The glorious fall leaves and the deep-blue sky and last night's full moon and the earthworms and microbes and constellations.

I know the one who made every piece of creation within reach of my fingers and my mind. I love him because he died for me and called me to have a special relationship with him. How can I not love the things he has made? How can I not want for them what he wants?

And "Why" Matters Too

Environmental stewardship. This is one of the most common phrases used today to talk about taking care of the earth. I like it, particularly because of the second word. A steward, according to my dictionary, is someone who takes care of something on behalf of someone else, and that is a very good way for us to think about our position between God the Creator and this place he has made.

As it happens, a landlord owns the house next to mine. Joe (not his real name) rents the apartments in it to tenants; he lives elsewhere in the city. He's a good landlord, and even does the mowing and snow removal himself. But he recently took a new job that has given him much less time to tend the property, and so he's in the process of looking for a property manager to take care of it for him. What he's looking for is a steward, someone who understands what he wants to do with his property and who will manage it accordingly.

Many people who use the term *stewardship* when talking about the environment do so without knowing or believing in God, and that is technically possible. A secular environmentalist may see herself as a steward and may teach and encourage what she calls environmental stewardship. She may mean that she wants to care for the earth on behalf of future generations. Or she might have in mind the earth and its creatures themselves. Either is a legitimate use of the concept of stewardship, and if you don't believe there is a God, stewardship of this kind is not only acceptable, it is necessary as an ethical foundation for environmental concern. We have to have a reason why we care.

But I'm a Christian, and I believe in God. For me, there is a richness and depth to the concept of stewardship that goes far, far beyond these. When I say that I'm a steward, I see myself as someone taking care of God's property on his behalf. He did not make this world for me—he made it for himself. But he put me—us—here to take care of it. Just as my friend Joe is looking for a property manager who will take care of his property with his goals in mind, you and I cannot be effective stewards of God's property until we understand what his goals are. This brings up the question, what are those goals? Why did he make it all in the first place? Why is it here?

The secularist—environmentalist or not—has no answer to this question. Maybe he doesn't need one. There is no "why"; the world just happens to be here. But even he would have to admit that this takes a bit of the wind out of the moral imperative that any ethic needs. If there is no "why," the world might just as easily happen not to be here. How long it lasts doesn't really matter one way or another. The secular stewardship ethic begins to falter. If there is no discernible reason for the existence of present or future generations of humans or for the presence of other species, acting as a steward on their behalf is a nice thought, but in the end it hardly matters. Who is really going to care if those future generations exist and prosper or fade in the dust of a silent and meaningless history?

As a Christian, I can legitimately ask why God made all that he made, and I can expect an answer. There is an answer that opens vistas of meaning for us, and that lends a powerful impetus to our role and actions as his property managers. That answer is implicit in one of the thoughts we have already seen in Colossians 1:16: he made it, not for us, but *for himself*.

A Temple Carved out of Space

Let's think about those first chapters of Genesis. Professor John Walton of Wheaton College suggests, with some other commentators, that the climax of God's creative acts is not on day six, when he creates man and woman (Genesis 1:27), but on day seven, when

God finished his work and blessed it. Walton writes,

> The cosmos is not set up with only people in mind. The cosmos is also intended to carry out a function related to God. On the seventh day we discover that God has been working to achieve a rest. This seventh day is not a theological appendix to the creation account, just to bring closure now that the main event of creating people has been reported. It intimates the purpose of creation and of the cosmos. God not only sets up the cosmos so that people will have a place; he also sets up the cosmos to serve as his temple. . . . He is making a rest for himself, a rest provided for by the completed cosmos. Inhabiting his resting place is the equivalent to being enthroned—it is connected to taking up his role as sovereign ruler of the cosmos. The temple simply provides a symbolic reality for this concept.[1]

"He also sets up the cosmos to serve as his temple." A temple in any culture is a place where people meet their God or gods, where they go to "worship." And whether those who enter the temple stand with hands uplifted as Orthodox Jews, kneeling with heads touching the ground as faithful Muslims, spinning prayer wheels as devout Hindus or "with every head bowed, every eye closed" as evangelical Christians, all are there to seek contact with deity. They are pursuing *relationship*.

And that, it turns out, is what the biblical story is about: God's relationship with . . . well, let's think about that for a minute. The standard ending to that statement would be "the human race." Certainly God created the human race "in his image," and that necessarily implies a very, very special relationship. We'll explore the implications of that special relationship in a bit. But that is not the only relationship on the table here. God expresses the same joyful "it is good" over the creation of the fish and the birds as he does over the creation of humans.

We have a bird feeder on our deck, and this year it seems to be attracting sparrows more than any other kind of bird. Sometimes there are twenty or thirty, flapping and fluttering and fighting with each other. Tiny, somewhat drab in color, a sparrow is not a very exciting bird. "Oh, it's just a sparrow" is the kind of comment that comes to mind. When a goldfinch or a cardinal or a redwing blackbird comes to visit, we sit up and take notice. But sparrows? Commonplace. Ordinary. Boring. And that is what makes these passages so interesting:

How lovely is your dwelling place, O LORD Almighty!
My soul yearns, even faints, for the courts of the LORD;
my heart and my flesh cry out for the living God.
Even the sparrow has found a home,
and the swallow a nest for herself, where she may
    have her young—
a place near your altar, O LORD Almighty, my King and my God.
Blessed are those who dwell in your house;
they are ever praising you. (Psalm 84:1-4)

[Jesus said,] "Are not two sparrows sold for a penny? Yet not one of them will fall to the ground apart from the will of your Father. And even the very hairs of your head are all numbered. So don't be afraid; you are worth more than many sparrows." (Matthew 10:29-31)

We interpret these passages, Matthew 10 in particular, as affirmations of how much God loves us. But please notice that the measure of God's love for us is how much he loves these other tiny creatures that he has made.

So God created creation for himself, and he created it to be a temple—a place in which he could pursue relationships with the creatures he created, not just with us human beings but with all of the creatures he had made.

Not Divine, but Sacred

One of the concerns I hear expressed among Christians when we talk about environmental issues is a fear of "worshiping" creation. In fact, an early book on this subject by Tony Campolo was called *How to Rescue the Earth Without Worshiping Nature*. Given our human tendency to worship anything but God, the concern is understandable. However, when we begin to see God's creation as a temple, this problem takes care of itself. Let me explain.

While working to aid Pakistan earthquake victims, I was based in Islamabad, Pakistan's capital city. My home and office was within sight of the Faisal Mosque, Islamabad's most prominent landmark and Pakistan's equivalent to the Washington National Cathedral. Located on the edge of the city, tucked against the Margalla Hills, this mosque is an important landmark and a popular and beautiful tourist attraction. I took visitors there on several occasions and would often walk the grounds alone early in the morning or in the evening.

The outside courtyard of Faisal Mosque is a marble-paved square about 150 yards on each side, and the worship area is comprised of a single hall approximately 80 yards square. Four minarets stand about 150 feet high at each corner of the main worship pavilion. Visitors are permitted to wander throughout the complex—the worship hall is closed except during prayer times—and tourists—men and women alike—are welcome, with just two conditions imposed on both Muslims and non Muslims: women should cover their heads, and everyone must remove their shoes. Why? Not because the structure is holy—a Muslim would shudder at the thought. Even a hint of idolatry is anathema in Islam. No, it is not holy, but it is sacred. It has been built and set apart for the worship of God and must therefore be treated with special respect.

You'll find the same thing if you visit the great cathedrals of Europe. You won't be asked to remove your shoes or cover your head, but the crowds of tourists, though they're on holiday, will move about quietly and will speak in low, respectful voices. We understand that these are special places—and we treat them with reverence.

So it is with God's creation. It is all holy ground, not just the area around Moses' burning bush. All of it is "worship space" because that is why God created it: to be a place where he could relate to his people.

We should, and we must, respect it and care for it, not because it is divine, but because it is sacred in the same way that a temple, cathedral or mosque is sacred. It is a place to meet God.

Do you ever wonder why it's easier to worship God outside, under the trees or on a mountaintop or beneath the stars on a summer night? It's because when we do that there, we are pursuing a relationship with the Creator in the place and in the way that he originally intended. Of course it's easier. It could hardly be otherwise!

Slave Masters or Choirmasters?

If all of creation is sacred, we have a potential problem. We are creatures who need to eat, who prefer to live in houses, who drive cars and wear clothes. Almost anything we do to live seems to add to the damage that the temple of creation is already sustaining.

Knowing that we have to live our lives and that we have to use creation to do so, some turn to the "dominion" teaching of Genesis 1 as the guiding rule for our behavior toward creation: "Let them rule [have dominion] over the fish of the sea and the birds of the air, over the livestock, over all the earth, and over all the creatures that move along the ground" (v. 26).

This has been used by some Christians to justify abuse of nature and by some non-Christians to accuse us of the same—sometimes justly, sometimes not. And this verse does seem to fly in the face of much that we have just discussed. But let's take a step back and think again.

Our desire as stewards is to appreciate what God's own goals for his world are, and the goal of our stewardship is, or should be, to make God's goals our own. Dominion—our rulership over the rest of creation—is simply the tool God has given us by which we can accomplish God's goals, not our own, in creation. When we understand God's purposes in creation properly, the apparent conflict disappears.

Let's pick up the worship motif again. As I've already said, we are not the only members of creation with whom the Creator has relationship. And it turns out that we are not the only actors in this great worship space. The author of Psalm 148 describes creation as an active participant in the worship of God. From the angels and the heavenly hosts, through sun and moon, waters above, sea creatures and ocean depths, through mountains, hills, small creatures and flying birds, to all of the human race,

> Praise the LORD from the earth, you great sea creatures
>   and all ocean depths,
> lightning and hail, snow and clouds, stormy winds that
>   do his bidding,
> you mountains and all hills, fruit trees and cedars,
> wild animals and all cattle, small creatures and flying birds,
> kings of the earth and all nations, you princes and all rulers
>   on earth,
> young men and maidens, old men and children.
> Let them praise the name of the LORD, for his name alone
>   is exalted;
> his splendor is above the earth and the heavens.
> (Psalm 148:7-13)

For more passages like this, read Psalms 19 and 104, and Job 38-40. Also consider the example of Jesus (Luke 4:42) and some of his teachings (Matthew 6:26 and following). It is a theme that repeats over and over. All creation bows in worship before the Creator.

This makes me think of a children's cartoon. You know the kind I mean: the furniture comes to life and the teapot dances with the teacups. God's temple isn't just a place for worship—it participates in that worship. This is what Jesus was talking about when his enemies complained about the way the crowds were treating him. Their enthusiastic praise seemed to them to border on blasphemy. Jesus' response to the complaints: "If they keep quiet, the stones will cry out" (Luke 19:40).

Creation, then, is both temple and choir, a place for worship as well as a participant in worship. This adds an important layer of meaning to the idea of dominion. The purpose of our leadership over creation is not that we might take anything we want from the riches of the earth for our own selfish purposes. No! We are the choirmasters. The purpose of our leadership is to help the cosmic choir to sing the heavenly song in the temple of creation.

One of my regrets is that I was born with little musical ability. I can appreciate good music, and I can carry the melody of a song if I have a lot of help around me. I do not have the ear/voice coordination that natural musicians have. But I have a friend with amazing musical abilities. He's been a pastor of music and worship in several large churches, and I've followed his career with interest. Tom (not his real name) is a classical, concert-level musician in his own right. But his real gift goes beyond his ability to produce music himself. His special talent is the way he can draw music out of others, often far beyond what they think they can accomplish. That, I believe, is the measure of a true choirmaster—someone who finds music in a choir that no one knew was there, not even the members of the choir themselves.

This is what *dominion* ought to mean. God has made us leaders and rulers in order that we might fulfill God's purposes by leading his cosmic choir in worship of himself—the Creator. This brings up an important question: How are we doing?

If you are a parent, you've probably had the experience of sitting through a "concert" in which your elementary-school children sang or played instruments. Often the concerts early in the school year are truly awful. We expect, though, that the end-of-year concerts will show improvement, and we expect that the pieces presented by older, more experienced student musicians will be, well, better than those done by beginners. If there were no improvement, we might judge the students themselves, but we'd be more likely to question the competence of their instructors, wouldn't we? How do we know if a music teacher, conductor or choirmaster has done her job? The music improves.

Back to the creation choir. How do you think the choir sounds now that we've been sitting in the choirmaster's chair for some thousands of years? Actually, the choir is dying. One in eight species of birds is threatened with extinction, as is one in four mammals and an unknown number of fish. Half of amphibians will not be on earth within the next decade or two. Can you imagine the choir of creation without frogs? At times, we've been guilty of driving creatures to extinction by overhunting. More often, we've simply removed their seats in the choir in order to make more room for our own. Places for creatures to live—biologists use the term *habitat*—disappear as the surface of the earth is covered by houses and pavement, highways and cities. Poisons filter into water, and whole mountains are destroyed to find veins of coal hidden beneath. This is dominion as domination, not dominion as stewardship. It is not improving the worship coming from the choir.

What kind of choirmasters are we, when the choir is being destroyed under our own hands?

The Book of God's Works

I recently talked with a friend who lives in North Carolina, across the street from a large Baptist church, the kind that is loudly committed to "saving the lost." Part of the church's property included a lovely section of woods with a stream. Mary (not her real name) doesn't worship at that church, but she used to spend a great deal of time in those woods, watching the birds, worshiping and praying. Last year the church needed more parking space. (You can see what's coming, can't you?) They removed the woods. While doing so, they failed to protect the stream during construction, and it was destroyed by the erosion and silt that resulted. True, more people can now park their cars and go inside to hear sermons about God's love. I can almost hear them singing, "His eye is on the sparrow, I know he cares for me." Meanwhile, outside their artificial sanctuary, God's great worship space has fewer places for sparrows to live, and one of God's chapels for prayer and worship is gone. Mary is not necessarily further from God because of this, but she certainly is not closer to the church across the street.

This incident is more common than not, and the lesson extends far

beyond church parking lots. You might not name Robert F. Kennedy
Jr. among your list of favorite prophets, but hear what he says in the
context of giving his own children experiences in God's creation:

> God communicates to us through each other and through orga-
> nized religion, through wise people and the great books,
> through music and art, but nowhere with such texture and
> forcefulness in detail and grace and joy as through creation. . . .
> When we destroy large resources, or when we cut off our access
> by putting railroads along river banks, by polluting so that peo-
> ple can't fish, or by making so many rules that people can't get
> out on the water, *it's the moral equivalent of tearing the last pages
> out of the last Bible on Earth.*[2]

When we fail to realize that God made creation to be one of the primary means by which human beings could come to know him, we
commit a grave error. Cal DeWitt often speaks of the value of an up-
bringing that allowed him to study the "book of God's word" and "the
book of God's works" together.[3] Psalm 19 is a hymn of praise to God
for revealing himself to us, and half of the psalm—the first half, incidentally—is given to God's revelation of himself in nature:

> The heavens declare the glory of God,
>   the skies proclaim the work of his hands.
> Day after day they pour forth speech;
>   night after night they display knowledge.
> There is no speech or language
>   where their voice is not heard.
> Their voice goes out into all the earth,
>   their words to the ends of the world. (Psalm 19:1-4)

Mary's church neighbors would have been rightly horrified if someone had desecrated several crates of Bibles. After all, those books are the
Word of God. But the woodland that succumbed to the bulldozer's
blade and the stream that no longer flows—God was speaking there too.

But let's be fair. Every church building that exists was put up at considerable cost to the plants and creatures that occupied that space be-fore the church came along. And most churches have parking lots. We can't build—churches, parking lots or houses—without the removal of trees and soil, and without causing the deaths of many of God's creatures. But clearly we must do so, to some extent at least.

So we have a dilemma. How do we live in a sacred temple when the very things we need to live (or to worship) seem to require dam-aging it in some way? This looks like it could be a complicated busi-ness. Thankfully, God did not leave us struggling alone with an im-possible dilemma. He came to us and showed us how we can live here as we will in heaven. He gave us a model—Jesus Christ, Son of God and Savior.

3

The Divine Consumer

In middle school and early high school, one of my children went through a serious "I have a crush" phase. Her idol was a singer with a popular contemporary Christian music group. An enormous poster hung over her bed, and every song he released was purchased, listened to, memorized and sung—over and over and over. One year the group was scheduled to sing in Chicago, just three or four hours from Madison. And it happened that the concert was scheduled close enough to my daughter's birthday that we could make her birthday party be a trip to see her idol on stage. So we bought the tickets. We even paid a bit extra so she and her friends could stand in line before the concert to meet him *in person.*

The great day came and everything, for once, went off without a hitch. We arrived at the concert venue in good time, stood in line, got our autographs, put in the earplugs (at least I did) and enjoyed the concert. It was a highlight of her young life. My ears are still ringing.

Now suppose—just suppose—that this singer had come to Madison, heard that his number-one fan lived in our house and decided to visit. What would have happened? There is no question that his visit would have lifted my daughter to the rafters and beyond. *Exalted* wouldn't begin to describe it. We would have been forbidden to use the chair he sat on, and there would have been no question of putting his cup or plate back into regular circulation. Everything that he touched would have been something special.

This is how we need to think of Jesus, the Son of God, coming to earth. We often think of his incarnation—becoming one of us—as *humiliation*. It is not a small thing for the all-powerful Creator of the universe to adopt the form of a creature, but that is exactly what happened:

> [Jesus,] being in very nature God, did not consider equality with God something to be grasped, but made himself nothing, taking the very nature of a servant, being made in human likeness. And being found in appearance as a man, he humbled himself and became obedient to death—even death on a cross. (Philippians 2:6-8)

Something else is just as important, though. When he *came down*, he *raised us up*, and all of creation as well. He lived here, in our house. When he walked down the street and sat in the shade of a tree, his presence was honoring and exalting to the dirt, the grass, the tree, the sky. If my daughter's idol, the singer, had actually come to our house, the effect would have been purely imaginary. Whatever fame and reputation this man had was purely ephemeral and already fading. He was no more worthy of praise and honor than I am—or than my daughter herself. Not so with Jesus. He made the dirt, the grass, the trees and the sky. When he arrived, his very presence affirmed the resounding pronouncement of Genesis 1: It is good—it's very good!

In the last chapter we saw creation as a temple, a cosmic worship space where a divine-human relationship can be pursued. In Jesus we see God himself walking the aisles of that temple, not just standing behind the altar. This is God as one of us: eating and drinking, laughing and playing, walking and talking, sleeping and working. Before we heard God say creation is good; now we see God himself enjoying creation. It must be good, and it must be worth taking care of.

The Son of the Earth at Home on Earth

One of Jesus' favorite names for himself is Son of Man. The title occurs twenty-eight times in Matthew's Gospel and with similar frequency in the other Gospels. This was not an unfamiliar phrase to Jesus' original listeners, though his use of it for himself would have certainly raised eyebrows. His fellow Jews would have thought of Ezekiel and Daniel, Old Testament prophets for whom "son of man" was an apocalyptic term. For them it spoke of the end of time, when God would bring history to an end and restore all things. But they might have also thought of Adam, the first "son of man." Adam's name comes from the Hebrew word *adamah*, earth. It is a reminder that "dust you are and to dust you will return" (Genesis 3:19).

There's no question that Jesus intended to connect his ministry with the end-times emphasis themes that "son of man" evoked for Ezekiel and Daniel. But the other, more down-to-earth meaning is also part of the picture he wants us to see. Bishop James Jones of Liverpool, England, pulls these two themes together for us in his book *Jesus and the Earth*:

> It is Jesus the Son of Man who has come down to the earth from heaven who holds together in himself both earthy things and heavenly things. The vision that is given to the prophet Ezekiel of God is of "one like Adam." This human picture of God is painted in the very earthy colors of the one hewn from the earth. Ezekiel's vision has standing at the center of the universe the figure of God drawn and depicted as an earthy human being. Here is the reality: Heaven and earth are not to be two separated realms for ever, divided by sin and evil, for the ultimate reality is an undivided world where all things whether on earth or in heaven hold together in Jesus (see Colossians 1). He is central to the earthing of heaven and to the heavening of earth. Earth and heaven belong together.[1]

The fact of Jesus' coming and his genuine earthiness reinforce what we've already seen. Creation must be cared for because God made it, because he made it as a sacred worship space in which we could meet him and because he himself walked along its paths, sat under its trees and used it for worship himself.

He Came Eating and Drinking

Knowing that Jesus walked this earth gives us a reason to take care of it. And watching him walk on the earth helps us to understand how we can live on this earth as creatures, and that it's okay to be a consumer of the good things God placed here. Bishop Jones again notes, "The fact is that Jesus Christ, the earthy revelation of God, exercises a material ministry. Jesus the Son of Man, like his earthy ancestor Adam, came into the world 'eating and drinking.'"[2]

Jesus was not an ascetic. In fact, people criticized him for just the opposite: "John came neither eating nor drinking, and they say, 'He has a demon.' The Son of Man came eating and drinking, and they say, 'Here is a glutton and a drunkard, a friend of tax collectors and "sinners"'" (Matthew 11:18-19).

God made the world beautiful. He made it to reflect his nature. He made it a place in which he could—and should—be worshiped. But he also made it tasty. The trees in the Garden were good for food. He intended that the fruit of creation be consumed by the creatures he placed in it. In fact, he set things up so creatures would have to eat other creatures in order to live: life consumes life, and thus life gives birth to life in a perpetual cycle of death and resurrection. There is no evidence, biblical or otherwise, that the food cycle we observe in nature today is a corruption of God's plan or a result of man's sin. It's all part of what God declared to be good.

DeWitt says, "We should enjoy, but must not destroy, creation's fruitfulness,"[3] and there are many examples in the Bible that show that God draws a line between the kind of use that is harvesting the fruit of creation and that which destroys its fruitfulness. Here are a few:

> When you lay siege to a city for a long time, fighting against it to capture it, *do not destroy its trees* by putting an ax to them, because you can eat their fruit. Do not cut them down. Are the trees of the field people, that you should besiege them? (Deuteronomy 20:19, emphasis added)

> If you come across a bird's nest beside the road, either in a tree

or on the ground, and the mother is sitting on the young or on the eggs, do not take the mother with the young. You may take the young, but be sure to let the mother go, so that it may go well with you and you may have a long life. (Deuteronomy 22:6-7)

When you enter the land I am going to give you, the land itself must observe a sabbath to the LORD. For six years sow your fields, and for six years prune your vineyards and gather their crops. But in the seventh year *the land is to have a sabbath of rest*, a sabbath to the LORD. Do not sow your fields or prune your vineyards. Do not reap what grows of itself or harvest the grapes of your untended vines. The land is to have a year of rest. (Leviticus 25:2-5, emphasis added)

In fact, there are stiff penalties for those who would destroy God's creation in the process of using what he has given:

Woe to you who add house to house
    and join field to field
till no space is left
    and you live alone in the land. (Isaiah 5:8)

    Your wrath has come.
The time has come for judging the dead,
    and for rewarding your servants the prophets
and your saints and those who reverence your name,
    both small and great—
and *for destroying those who destroy the earth*.
(Revelation 11:18, emphasis added)

Jesus came "eating and drinking" and showed us by his example that we can do the same without fear or guilt. God made us to be consumers, and it's okay to use the fruit of God's creation. He intended that we do so. But we dare not extend our license to consume to the point where our consumption destroys, degrades or diminishes creation's ability to be fruitful. That is contrary to Jesus' example and exposes us to God's wrath in ways we would rather not experience.

A Carpenter, Not a Gardener

So Jesus came eating and drinking. He also came working. As with other Jewish rabbis of his day, he was trained in an occupation. His father was a carpenter, and he became one too (Mark 6:3). Think about this with me. Jesus worked with wood, one of the most common materials of the earth. He cut down living trees, sawed and planed, chiseled and shaped the wood, and produced things for people. He almost certainly sold what he made for a profit. This would have made him a businessman as well.

This is fascinating. When my organization works with poor farmers in Africa, we often teach that God was the First Farmer, for he planted a garden. We do this intentionally; we want farmers to understand that in tending and caring for the earth, they are engaged in a God-ordained and God-glorifying occupation. It's honorable to be a farmer, and if you are one, I would pause here to salute you and would certainly shake your hand if we were together in the same room.

We might expect that when God arrived on earth, he would have chosen to be a gardener or a farmer. He would have worked the soil, as the first Adam did. This would fit neatly into what we read in Genesis about tending and caring for the earth. But no. Jesus comes on the scene as a carpenter and a businessman. He is the closest thing to an engineer that his society had. In the process of conducting his trade, he had to use the produce of creation. Living trees had to be chopped down to give him material with which to work. Further, he likely made not just furniture but farm implements, including yokes to harness oxen (see Matthew 11:30) and plows for them to pull through the fields. He might have made gates for farmers to pen in their sheep or other domesticated animals. Or a table for a butcher's shop. As a carpenter, Jesus' trade would have supported many aspects of the agricultural enterprises that sustained his community.

It would be easy to take from the lessons of the last chapter an idea that we ought to be tiptoeing through the temple of creation, taking care not to disturb any of the other creatures for fear we might disrupt their worship of their Creator. That is not possible. We have to eat, and we have already seen that this and every other activity of our lives has some impact on the rest of creation. Jesus shows us that "tiptoeing through the tulips" is not only not possible, it's not necessary. He would be the first to tell us that cutting down all the trees in a forest is wrong, that fishing a lake until there are no fish left is a sin and that a manufacturing process that results in water that poisons fish and air that causes human cancers is an obscenity and a blasphemy. But he would not tell us not to cut down any trees or take any fish. He is Son of the Earth, remember, and he shows us by his example that it's okay for us to involve ourselves—responsibly—in using the earth to manufacture, buy and sell from each other.

It would be nice to go back to the Garden of Eden, to be able to consume the fruit of creation in the peaceful harmony God originally intended. But we can't go back. It's not possible. There are simply too many human beings on earth to allow us to "go back to nature." One or two people camping in the woods can relieve themselves behind the bushes, and there are no problems. In fact, the plants in the area were designed by God to accept and recycle the waste products of animals like ourselves and benefit from them. But a permanent camping area with fifty or a hundred sites had better have permanent toilet facilities with a septic tank, or the results will be disastrous.

Unfortunately, you might say, the results are pretty disastrous now. It's fine to say that Jesus' example allows us to be consumers and workers and business people. But to say, "Just be a responsible consumer," may be like telling an alcoholic to drink responsibly. Responsible consuming is not what we see when we look at the world today, and even those of us who have struggled with these things for years find ourselves coming up short. We are consuming what we don't need and not enjoying it at all. We work without satisfaction for years to pay off debts for things we bought but didn't need, while millions of others work themselves to death and barely have enough to survive from one day to the next. And creation suffers and groans under the burden of such consumption.

It looks like we need more than an example. We need something to fix whatever is wrong.

4

Diagnosis: Sin

For more than fifteen years, my wife, Susanna, has suffered from a variety of physical ailments that for a long time defied diagnosis. We went from doctor to doctor. We researched and studied. We learned to manage her symptoms, sometimes with medical help, sometimes without. We had some helpful and sympathetic doctors and some who, frankly, should not have been practicing medicine. But we always felt we were playing catch-up, because neither we nor our medical team could get a handle on the underlying causes. What was the disease? If we knew that, we could, perhaps, begin to make progress.

Eight years ago we changed our medical plan. Because we were moving from one HMO to another, we had to change our entire medical team. We never made a better decision in our lives. With new people looking at Susanna's history, it seemed as if overnight we had a new treatment plan, new medications and a greatly improved quality of life. How did this happen? One of our new doctors gave us something we had not had before: a diagnosis. He was able to identify the disease at the root of all of the symptoms. With that new understanding came more tools, more appropriate use of the tools we already had and a much, much better outcome.

A good diagnosis is half the cure. And our story illustrates a major difficulty with the modern environmental crisis. In chapter one I summarized several aspects of that crisis: it's a global crisis, a population crisis, a prosperity crisis, a poverty crisis and a political crisis. But these are like Susanna's symptoms: they are evidence of a disease, but they don't describe the disease itself. We can look at each one and we can try to manage them, but they don't tell us what the underlying problem is. Without that diagnosis, we're doomed to a series of Band-Aid efforts that never get to the root of the problem. Without a diagnosis, there's no cure. And without a cure, there's no hope.

"We Didn't Mean To"

If you are a parent, you've heard the crash as a ball sails through a window or as two children playing tag in the living room collide with the priceless lamp sent by Aunt Jane twenty-three years ago. What do you always hear next? "But, Mom, we didn't mean to."

That phrase echoes down the halls of human history. Jared Diamond's book *Collapse* is a study of a number of civilizations and societies from prehistoric times to the present that encountered difficulties—often environmental—and disappeared. A classic example is the civilization on Easter Island in the South Pacific. Diamond writes,

> The overall picture for Easter is the most extreme example of forest destruction in the Pacific, and among the most extreme in the world: the whole forest gone, and all of its tree species extinct. . . . I have often asked myself, "What did the Easter Islander who cut down the last palm tree say while he was doing it?"[1]

I suspect he would have said what the children said about Aunt Jane's lamp: "We didn't mean to."

Have you read Dr. Seuss's book *The Lorax*? It's now more than thirty years old, but it's worth reading again. The Once-ler, a business-type creature, faces off against the Lorax. Once-ler discovers Truffula trees and proceeds to chop them down to make Thneeds—useless things that "everyone needs." The Lorax "speaks for the trees, which you seem to be chopping as fast as you please." You can guess where the story goes. The last tree is chopped down, and Once-ler is left amid crumbling factories beneath a smelly sky to wonder why and how all this happened:

I meant no harm. I most truly did not.
But I had to grow bigger. So bigger I got.
I biggered my factory. I biggered my roads.
I biggered my wagons. I biggered the loads
of the Thneeds I shipped out. I was shipping them forth
to the South! To the East! To the West! To the North!
I went right on biggering . . . selling more Thneeds.
And I biggered my money, which everyone needs.[2]

"I meant no harm." "We didn't mean to." No one does. But we can't seem to stop ourselves. Why?

Consumerism Is a Spiritual Problem

Some time ago, Dave Roberts, a writer for online magazine *Grist*, addressed the issue of materialism and consumerism—the same thing Dr. Seuss seemed to be trying to get at. This is what Dave had to say:

> What's striking about the "frenzied grasping for stuff" is not the stuff but the frenzied grasping. We seem perpetually unfulfilled, convinced that just a slightly bigger house or faster car or more flattering pair of jeans or higher-capacity mp3 player will fill the holes inside us. I don't write this off to simple greed. And though there is an advertising industry devoted to stoking and exacerbating these feelings, I don't think it could create them from whole cloth. *Why the perpetual, gnawing sense of dissatisfaction?*[3]

Several years earlier, John DeGraaf of PBS and KCTS Television (Seattle) produced a television program and book called *Affluenza*. Here's DeGraaf's definition of the term he created:

> *affluenza*, n. 1. The bloated, sluggish and unfulfilled feeling that results from efforts to keep up with the Joneses. 2. An epidemic of stress, overwork, waste and indebtedness caused by dogged pursuit of the American Dream. 3. An unsustainable addiction to economic growth.[4]

These are not Christian commentators, but they come close to an accurate diagnosis. Roberts in particular is asking the right question: "Why the perpetual, gnawing sense of dissatisfaction?" I can answer him with one word—*sin*—but it needs some explanation, because I'm not using it as most people might. Most of us will think of sin of something that someone does. Murderers sin. Bank robbers sin. Politicians who lie sin. The kid running into Aunt Jane's lamp sinned—maybe (he deserves his day in court; it might have been his sister chasing him). But when I buy a new MP3 player or a new car? How is that a sin?

Clearly there's a bit more to this concept of sin. Let's take a short detour back to the beginning of the story, to the Garden of Eden.

Relationships Falling Like Dominoes

The story starts, well, nicely. God's new creatures, Adam and Eve, are living in a garden given them by the Creator himself. It's a place of beauty, of bounty, of peace. Eat what you want, when you want. Sleep anywhere. Paradise indeed! Just that one small limitation: don't touch the tree in the middle of the garden. And you know the story. Enter the serpent, allow doubt to creep into these naive (in the best sense) and trusting minds, and the rest is history. She ate; he ate—and we've been on a downhill track ever since.

Let's look at the scene for a minute. There were Adam and Eve, fruit juice still on their chins. They "heard the sound of the LORD God as he was walking in the Garden in the cool of the day, and they hid from the LORD God" (Genesis 3:8). They heard the sound of God in the Garden—what I hear is the sound of relationships shattering. Like dominoes, they fall one after another.[5]

> 1. *Their relationship with God was broken.* Implicit in their relationship with God was his right to command them and their obligation to obey. Having dispensed with their side of the arrangement, they could not face him, and so they hid. Separation. Alienation. Because they were created to live with—and

within—God, disruption of this primary relationship led immediately to inner turmoil. And . . .

2. *Their relationship with themselves was broken.* Adam said to
God, "I was afraid because I was naked" (v. 10). Volumes have
been written on this short phrase. It could mean many things; at
the very least, it shows that people who had been at peace with
themselves are now filled with guilt and shame. There's an inner
turmoil that was absent before Adam disobeyed. And because
each of these sinners could not live with themselves, they could
not live with each other. Then . . .

3. *Their relationship with each other was broken.* It doesn't take long
for the first marital argument to break out: "The woman you put
here with me—she gave me some fruit from the tree, and I ate it"
(v. 12). Whether the discord is between spouses, parents and children, neighbors on the street or heads of state about to go to war,
it all started here. Shattered community. Being unable to live with
each other, it's not surprising that they were no longer able to live
in harmony with other members of God's creation. And, finally, . . .

4. *Their relationship with the rest of creation was broken.* God pro-
nounced his curse on the serpent, on the woman and on the
man. In pronouncing judgment on Adam, God said,

Cursed is the ground because of you;
    through painful toil you will eat of it
    all the days of your life.
It will produce thorns and thistles for you,
    and you will eat the plants of the field.
By the sweat of your brow
    you will eat your food
until you return to the ground,
    since from it you were taken;
For dust you are,
    and to dust you will return. (vv. 17-19)

This is presented as a criminal judgment, but Adam's doom is also the logical and inevitable outcome of what has gone before. He was created by God to live in harmony with the rest of creation. That harmony depended on an ongoing relationship with the Creator. He broke that relationship, and disharmony—disease, thorns, thistles—followed as surely as night follows day.

Sin as Sinfulness

Adam and Eve's disobedience, breaking their relationship with God, created a new condition we can call *sinfulness*. This is sin-as-something-one-is as opposed to sin-as-something-one-does. Adam and Eve started us down this path, but every one of us has followed. Sinfulness makes us unfulfilled and dissatisfied because we don't have God. It drives us to selfishness and greed. It creates in us a compulsion to find satisfaction and meaning anywhere we can. Sinfulness is the virus that carries the affluenza disease DeGraaf identified, that infects us with Roberts's "perpetual, gnawing sense of dissatisfaction," that fills shopping malls with people who already own more than they can use and owe more than they can pay off. The consumer-driven lifestyle is not the disease—it is a symptom of this deeper problem, sinfulness. As is the poisoned air that comes from a factory whose owners have neglected to install appropriate filters. And so is war of every kind, with the loss of human life and the devastation of God's creation that inevitably results.

Let's get back to the purchase of an MP3 player I mentioned earlier. Buying it is *not necessarily* a sin. But it might be. If you're buying it as a gift for your brother, who is about to ship out for an overseas tour of duty, no, it's not a sin. But if you're getting it just because it's newer and bigger and better than your old one or you just don't know why you're buying it but it might make you forget that fight with your boyfriend and it's either an MP3 player or that new top that you saw over at Macy's—if that is the case, then yes, it's a sin.

We begin to understand why the environmental crisis is proving to be such a tough problem to solve. The stress we put on God's creation is caused in large part by our sinfulness as well as our sins. It is what we *are* that drives us to *do* what we do. Most of the solutions proposed for the environmental crisis are either technological (develop and implement "green" manufacturing) or regulatory (tax or prohibit what we don't want, subsidize what we do want). But neither technology nor regulation will solve a problem that originates in the human heart. We need changes in behavior. We need transformed lives. For it turns out that sin is far more than an academic question. Sin has consequences.

The Wages of (Environmental) Sin

It was an historic evening at our house. Our son had just received his driver's license and was driving his sister to their youth group meeting for the first time. After giving all of the usual parental admonitions, we set a nine o'clock curfew. I knew what to expect. Sure enough, nine o'clock came and there was no car in the driveway. 9:01. 9:02. At 9:03, we heard car doors slam and steps on the front sidewalk. The infraction was hardly serious—just three minutes—but if you had been there you might have thought my children had been an hour late. I threw the book at them. Why? I wasn't angry. No, I wanted to communicate a very important principle to a young man (and his sister), who were about to enter a world of high speed and great danger: *Rules matter.*

As a family, we attempted to have firm but reasonable rules, and we often debated and sometimes modified those rules as our children got older. If you listen to our older children, we modified them far too much for the younger ones, something that is, I'm afraid, a universal tendency as parents get older and wiser and just plain tired. There's no question that sometimes we were too strict and other times too lenient. However, the guiding principle never changed. The rules had to be obeyed. Sin has consequences.

This is a fundamental principle in the Bible and in life. God created us to live in harmony with him and in a comfortable web of relationships in his creation. Breaking those relationships—sin—results in consequences. "The wages of sin is death" (Romans 3:23) is a phrase known to almost every evangelical Christian, and here it means eternal, spiritual death. Apart from God's grace, sin leads to eternal punishment.

But we don't have to wait until death to see the consequences of sin. Sins that affect our bodies (smoking, drugs, overeating) often result in pain and suffering now. And sins that affect God's creation often result in disastrous consequences. In the last chapter I made reference to this verse from Isaiah 5: "Woe to you who add house to house and join field to field till no space is left and you live alone in the land" (v. 8).

Take a look at the verses that immediately follow:

> The LORD Almighty has declared in my hearing:
> "Surely the great houses will become desolate,
>   the fine mansions left without occupants.
> A ten-acre vineyard will produce only a bath [about six gallons]
>   of wine,
>   a homer [about six bushels] of seed only an ephah [about half a
>   bushel] of grain." (vv. 9-10)

Isaiah's language of spiritual judgment describes what we can easily recognize as ecological consequences: overcrowding and overworking of agricultural land will inevitably lead to diminished yields, and economic collapse will follow as night follows day. Call it a judgment or call it an environmental consequence. It doesn't matter which: Rules matter. Sin has consequences. Environmental problems are sin problems.

What we're seeing in the world today is ample evidence that rules matter. We can't disobey with impunity. There are limits to how far we can push our rebellion against God when it comes to his creation. After too much abuse, the land will refuse to produce crops. The ocean will stop yielding fish. Wells will dry up. *Rules matter. Sin has consequences.*

My son wasn't happy when I called him on his three-minute infraction, but he never violated a curfew again. He learned that rules do matter, but he also learned that within the rules there could be peace and freedom. He learned to call if he was going to be late. He explained; we negotiated. He learned to live within the rules—and that there was grace available as well.

But getting back inside God's rules is not so simple. Who do we call to say we're late and we're lost? It's good and necessary to learn what the rules are—that is the role of ecology and biology. And it's fine to say that God's rules for living in his creation are good and that we need to get back inside that web of relationship. But we can't. The web has been broken. Someone else is going to have to help.

5

Reversing the Curse

It is March 2006. I'm in Kenya, at the Brackenhurst International Conference Center near Nairobi. More than 260 church and denominational leaders have gathered from all over East Africa for a four-day conference called "God and Creation." These men and women have come together to discuss and learn about issues related to the environmental crisis as it affects Kenya and East Africa. Kenya is experiencing one of the worst droughts in its modern history, and environment is on everyone's mind. We've had plenty of practical workshops on farming and irrigation. Participants have learned about tree planting and water harvesting.

But this has not been a typical environmental conference. Much of our time has been spent in worship and Bible study, and now, in the final session, I'm holding a document that I'm going to ask every participant to read together and then to sign. But first I ask for prayer. And the prayers begin to pour out. In English, Kiswahili, Kikuyu. And in other tribal languages. I understand few of these, but I know these are prayers of thanksgiving to God for his grace and love. Prayers of confession for sinning against him in how we have treated our land. Prayers for help as we seek to learn to manage our farms in ways that will bring glory to his name.

And then, with a delightful mix of African, European and American accents, we read our covenant together.

> We believe in one God, the Creator, Owner and Sustainer
> of all things. . . .

We believe that God calls us to be good stewards of His creation. . . .

We believe the environmental crisis emerging in East Africa poses a critical threat to our future. . . .

We confess that the church has responded poorly to this issue. (See the full declaration, "Mobilizing God's People to Care for God's Creation," appendix 1.)

If you had been visiting from another environmental organization, you might have been confused. What does this religiosity have to do with the environment? We have a practical crisis on our hands. Surely what is needed is trees—training—planning—funding. But prayer? What does prayer have to do with anything?

Reconciliation Before Restoration

I've established that the cause of the environmental crisis is our sin-fulness: it's a spiritual problem, and we have to have a solution that addresses that problem. It's no good trying to dress up the same old solutions with new language. If it's a "spiritual" problem, it has to have a "spiritual" solution.

This is what Paul is talking about in Colossians 1, a key passage we cannot avoid coming back to over and over: "For God was pleased to have all his fullness dwell in him [Jesus], and through him to recon-cile to himself all things, whether things on earth or things in heaven, by making peace through his blood, shed on the cross" (vv. 19-20). If the problem is alienation (read: separation), the solution is reconcili-ation. The central message of the Bible is that God accomplished rec-onciliation—we also use the term *redemption*—through Jesus' death on the cross. All of us who call ourselves Christians or Christ-followers are in agreement on this point.

But what does it mean for God to "reconcile to himself *all things*"? The sentence I quoted above is part of a longer paragraph in which the exact phrase occurs five times, and similar wording four more times, for a total of nine occurrences in one short paragraph:

He is the image of the invisible God, the firstborn over *all creation.* For by him *all things* were created: *things in heaven and on earth,* visible and invisible, whether thrones or powers or rulers or authorities; *all things* were created by him and for him. He is before *all things,* and in him *all things* hold together. And he is the head of the body, the church; he is the beginning and the firstborn from among the dead, so that *in everything* he might have the supremacy. For God was pleased to have all his fullness dwell in him, and through him to reconcile to himself *all things,* whether *things on earth or things in heaven,* by making peace through his blood shed on the cross. (vv. 15-20, emphasis added)

The "all things" that were created are the "all things" that are being held together, and the "all things" that are being reconciled through the blood of Jesus.

There's a worship song we occasionally sing with a line that goes something like this: "He [God] thought of me alone." It's a nice thought, but nothing could be further from the truth. What God thought of when he sent his Son to die on the cross was not "me alone" or "you alone"—it was nothing less than creation-wide redemption. It was a plan that would reach to every corner of the universe and that would reclaim every square inch damaged by our sin. The implications for the environmental crisis are obvious: creation damaged by our sin will be restored by our redemption.

But that's a bit of a leap. How does it happen?

Putting the Dominoes Back in Place

Like many kids, young and old, I used to enjoy playing with dominoes. Not playing the game, you understand, but playing with the tiles. Setting them up in long chains, and when all was ready, carefully knocking the first one over. If all went according to plan, each domino would knock the next one in the line, and one by one, all would fall over. In the last chapter, I used that image to describe the series of relationships shattered by Adam and Eve's disobedience. As we think of how these relationships are restored by redemption through Jesus, the domino imagery is useful again. As the domino tiles fall, each pushes on the next, and eventually all are lying down. But if you want to pick them up, you have to start with the first one that fell over, not with the last. *They have to be set up in the order in which they fell.* The same is true as we begin to restore relationships broken by sin.

Just as each broken relationship caused the next one to break, so each restored relationship makes possible the restoration of the next. The order is important. Here's what I mean:

1. *We begin with our relationship with God being restored.* Theologians call this "regeneration." You may want to call it "personal salvation." It's what Jesus meant when he said we must be born again (see John 3:3). It's what happens when each one of us, becoming aware of our sins and our sinfulness (see chapter five) comes to God, asking for forgiveness and accepting his gift of grace and forgiveness. This is "peace with God," and it makes inner peace possible as well. And

2. *Our relationship to ourselves is restored.* Adam and Eve revealed inner turmoil when they became aware that they were naked. Similarly you and I experience a combination of guilt, shame, anxiety, discouragement and despair because of our sinfulness. An important part of the Christian experience is the gift of inner peace as, having accepted God's forgiveness, we can be at peace with ourselves. Trusting him, we can release anxiety about the future. Knowing him, we have purpose for living. The agent of this healing process is the Holy Spirit, and theologically we call it "sanctification." Inner peace and healing then set up the conditions needed for the next stage. People at peace with themselves find it possible to live peacefully with each other. Then . . .

3. *Our relationship with other people is restored.* Sin and inner turmoil lead to family and community conflict; redemption and in-

ner peace are the foundation on which we can build a network of authentic relationships in marriages, in families, and with people all around us—church, work, school. The Bible's word for God-centered community is *koinonia,* and it's the basis for the institution we call the church. (I'll have a lot more to say about the church in the next chapter.) Learning to live together in peaceful and happy social networks becomes a foundation for restoring our relationship with nature and the created order. And, finally, . . .

4. Our relationship with the rest of creation is restored.

I expect you'll agree with me that the restoration of the first three relationships is a natural and expected result of God's redemption. Relationships restored are an indication that a person is a follower of Jesus. You can tell by looking at her life. People who have their sins forgiven *should* experience inner peace and joy. They *should* have marriages and families and community relationships that exhibit the grace and peace of God. This is what many of us understand not only the Christian life but also the church to be all about, as we will see in chapters still to come.

Conversely, lack of progress in any of these relationships is a spiritual warning sign. For example, Peter tells husbands to treat their wives well, "so that nothing will hinder your prayers" (1 Peter 3:7). There is a direct correlation between a husband's relationship with God, as measured in the effectiveness of his prayers here on earth, and how he treats his wife. The same is true of parents and children.

But what about my relationship to creation? The same logic could mean that how I treat my dog and how I treat my lawn and how I dispose of batteries is a measure of my faith, an indication of my spiritual health. Might there be a correlation between my relationship with God and how I treat his world? This is a leap few of us have taken, but it seems hard to avoid.

If our relationship with creation is broken because of sin (and it is),

Cursed is the ground because of you; through painful toil you will eat of it all the days of your life. It will produce thorns and this-tles for you. (Genesis 3:17, emphasis added)

And if the redemption that brought us salvation is intended to restore that relationship (and it is),

God was pleased to have all his fullness dwell in him, and through him *to reconcile to himself all things,* whether things on earth or things in heaven, by making peace through his blood, shed on the cross. (Colossians 1:19-20, emphasis added)

And if nonhuman creation is waiting with anticipation for that rela-tionship to be restored (and it is),

the creation waits in eager expectation for the sons of God to be re-vealed. For the creation was subjected to frustration, not by its own choice, but by the will of the one who subjected it, in hope that the creation itself will be liberated from its bondage to decay and brought into the glorious freedom of the children of God. We know that the whole creation has been groaning as in the pains of childbirth right up to the present time. (Romans 8:19-22, emphasis added)

Then the conclusion is unavoidable. Our relationship to creation *is* part of the same process as all of the others. And just as with the other relationships, a positive relationship here is a sign of spiritual growth and maturity—and a poor or negative relationship is a warning sign of problems. In fact, how I treat my dog and my lawn and how I dis-pose of my waste really is a measure of how well God's redemption is working in my life.

A Peace That Passes Understanding

There's a Hebrew word that describes the fulfillment of restored rela-tionships that God's reconciliation is seeking to accomplish: *shalom.* In its simplest definition it means "peace," and is, to this day, in daily use throughout the Middle East as part of the most common greeting. Hebrew, Arabic, Persian, Urdu and several other languages all use some variant of this word. I grew up in Pakistan with the ancient (and biblical) greeting and response "Salaam aleikum . . . W'aleikum sa-laam" in my brain. "Peace to you . . . And to you also, peace."

The "peace" of shalom is much more than lack of conflict. Think of a quiet evening marked by calm, stillness and tranquility. You're sit-ting on the porch of a farmhouse, with fields and woods stretched out in front of you. The noise of the highway is dying away, the sun is set-ting, and the ducks quack quietly down on the pond. Overhead, stars begin to appear one by one. It's a peaceful setting, and there's a feeling of rest and completeness. This is a glimpse of what God has in mind when he holds out *shalom* as a goal and a promise:

> The LORD bless you
>   and keep you;
> the LORD make his face shine upon you
>   and be gracious to you;
> the LORD turn his face toward you
>   *and give you peace.* (Numbers 6:24-26, emphasis added)

Shalom is complete restoration and healing: the curse is reversed, and all of the dominoes are set back up; God's original web of relation-ships is again intact; and we human beings are fulfilling our role as God's choirmasters, living out our lives in obedience and worship, with all creation around us singing his praises. That is full redemption!

But What About the Rapture?

But—but—"full redemption" can occur only at the end of history, when Jesus returns, when the "first earth" and "first heaven" are re-placed by a new heaven and earth, when "the old order of things has passed away" (Revelation 21:4). Right?

Passages like this one have been the Achilles heel of Christians try-ing to engage in environmental stewardship:

> The present heavens and earth are reserved for fire, being kept

for the day of judgment and destruction of ungodly men. . . .

But the day of the Lord will come like a thief. The heavens will disappear with a roar; the elements will be destroyed by fire, and the earth and everything in it will be laid bare.

Since everything will be destroyed in this way, what kind of people ought you to be? You ought to live holy and godly lives as you look forward to the day of God and speed its coming. That day will bring about the destruction of the heavens by fire, and the elements will melt in the heat. But in keeping with his promise we are looking forward to a new heaven and a new earth, the home of righteousness. (2 Peter 3:7, 10-13)

This picture—so well depicted in C. S. Lewis's *The Last Battle*—has tended to muddle our thinking as Christians about the earth. If "it's all going to burn up anyway," it seems not to matter much what we do with the earth. And since Peter tells us to "speed its coming," maybe we're doing God a favor by helping that final destruction along.

Evangelical denial of the environmental crisis has, until recently, been widespread. This still seems odd to me. It doesn't take into consideration, for example, that a careful reading of Revelation strongly suggests a parallel between the predicted plagues of the last days and the devastation we can see in the world now that is due to widespread environmental devastation. In Revelation 8, John describes this scene: "The third angel sounded his trumpet, and a great star, blazing like a torch, fell from the sky on a third of the rivers and on the springs of water—the name of the star is Wormwood. *A third of the waters turned bitter, and many people died from the waters that had become bitter*" (vv. 10-11, emphasis added).

You could argue that this verse is being fulfilled right now in Bangladesh. There's a little-known crisis developing there, in which thousands of wells that were drilled over the last fifteen years appear to be poisoned with naturally occurring arsenic from the ground water. Low-level arsenic poisoning takes decades to develop, and only now is it becoming clear that millions and millions of people have been drinking poisoned water for decades and are almost certainly doomed to slow and painful deaths. The World Bank calls it one of the worst public-health disasters in history.

One would think those of us who really believe the pages of Revelation (and yes, you can count me among them) would accept the realities of the environmental crisis and the most dire predictions of climate change disaster by saying, "Of course! This is what we've read about and what we were expecting!" Why would we deny something in the newspaper that we've been reading about in the Bible all our lives?

Why, indeed. Most of us did not expect that we would have to deal with such situations personally, still less that we would find ourselves in the awkward position of actually contributing to Revelation-like plagues through our own actions and lifestyles. The rapture was supposed to save us from this! But if this connection between current events and biblical prophecy is true—if we are seeing the beginnings of the end of history as described in the Bible—where does that leave us?

First, there's a possibility that the traditional interpretation of Peter's prophecy is, not to put too fine a point on it, wrong. Steven Bouma-Prediger is one of several recent commentators suggesting that Peter is describing a "cleansing fire" rather than a destructive fire and that his allusion to Noah's flood might suggest that the "new earth" we're looking forward to could in fact be this old earth, cleansed and renewed. God might be, in Bouma-Prediger's view, "the great recycler."[1] It's not my job to try to untangle these kinds of exegetical debates, nor am I qualified to do so. But we should be aware of the possibility that a passage as critical as this one might not say exactly what many of us always thought it did.

But let's assume, for the time being anyway, that the traditional reading of Peter's prophecy is correct—that this present world will burn up and vanish in a mighty cosmic cataclysm, along with the destruction of the heavenly bodies, to be replaced with a new earth and a new heaven where all will be perfect. Where does that leave us? Answer: it doesn't change anything! It doesn't matter! The process of redemption that we've been exploring will and must carry on, regardless of whether this old earth is destined for fire in six months or six centuries. In fact, Peter says as much: "Since everything will be destroyed in this way, what kind of people ought you to be? You ought to live holy and godly lives as you look forward to the day of God and speed its coming" (2 Peter 3:11). Even if the traditional view—"it's all going to burn up anyway"—turns out to be correct, Peter sees this as a reason for being more careful about how we live, not less so.

As I was writing these pages, I found myself attending a most unexpected funeral—that of the twenty-five-year-old daughter of some dear friends. I'll call her Sarah. She was suddenly taken to the hospital, and within four days she was dead, apparently from viral encephalitis. The funeral service was sad, as one would have expected, but it was also triumphant. Family and friends shared the devastation of a life cut short, but also comforted each other with the confidence and promise that her life was not over and that she and we would meet again.

I can't help wonder what would have happened if Sarah had been told, say a month earlier, that she had just one month to live. What would she have said or done differently? I'm sure she would have found time to spend with the people she loved and would have made sure her family and friends knew how much she loved them. She might have made a list of "last things" to do—a trip to her favorite ice cream parlor, a last walk in her favorite park.

I'm sure she would not have used her last month running riot, doing the things she had avoided all of her young life. I don't think she would have spent the nights getting drunk, looking for quick sex or getting high on every drug she could find. I don't think she would have become the wildest driver on the Chicago tollway system or spent her last hours in the mall maxing out credit cards she would never have to repay. She could have thought, *It doesn't matter what I do, because I'm going to die in a month anyway,* but I don't think she would have. Few of us, faced with such a situation, would think like that. We would want to make the most of every minute right up to the end, and that would drive us away from frivolity and disaster and toward meaning and substance.

Do you see the connection? Even if this earth is doomed for destruction and replacement, we can't treat it casually because of that. Rather, like Sarah, we should find ourselves living even more carefully, taking better care—simply because our time here is limited.

Rejoining the Celestial Orchestra

Let me try to pull the various themes of this chapter together with one more story.

I was waiting on the high-school gym bleachers, squeezed in with hundreds of other parents, while the gymnasium floor slowly filled with more than nine hundred young people. Each one held a violin, viola or other instrument in one hand, a bow in the other. Madison's annual All-City Strings Festival was about to begin.

We'd been astounded when we moved to Madison to discover a wonderful program simply called "Elementary Strings." Beginning in fourth grade, every child who wants to can learn to play a stringed instrument. The numbers drop in the older grades, but as many as 50 percent of fourth-graders took part in the program at one time. The program culminates each year with the spring Strings Festival. After weeks of memorization and practice (no sheet music allowed) students from all the elementary and middle schools come together to form one giant orchestra on a Saturday morning. This was that Saturday.

The conductor raised his baton. Nine hundred bows came to attention. And we were enveloped in waves of beautiful, harmonious music. It was powerful. It was beautiful. And it really was music. It was unbelievable.

It reminded me of how God's redemption works in the context of his creation. God is the celestial conductor. And more, he's the instrument maker, he's the composer—and he's the audience as well. We human beings are key players in this celestial orchestra, so we're like the violins. But there are a lot of other instruments as well. Each of us has an instrument, made for us by God. We have a score: his revealed will to us. And like the children in that gym, our goal is to make music.

Successful music depends on each one of us doing our part: we have to learn to play, and we have to keep our instruments in tune. (First we have to have the instruments fixed—that's the restoration of the four key relationships already discussed.) We have to keep our eyes on the conductor, and of course, we have to follow the score. And God participates in the process from beginning to end: He gave each one of us instruments to play. He has taught us, given us the score and stands at our side day by day, pointing out parts we need to work on. He works with us to keep in tune and in time with his heavenly music.

It's a wonderful picture—and two things I have already talked about jump out.

There is a difference between sin and sinfulness that matters. We sin by doing wrong things, and it is as if we are playing the wrong notes. But *our sinfulness* is the something that's wrong inside us; it's like having an instrument that's out of tune because it's so broken that it *can't* be tuned. Even if we play the right notes, the music will be awful. Whether the issues are broken family relationships or a watershed devastated by erosion, we can know what the problems are (the wrong notes), but we still can't play in tune or on key. Our instruments have to be fixed. This is the mysterious work of the Holy Spirit at the core of the entire process of redemption. No amount of trying to be good will ever be good enough. Redemption means God has fixed our instruments, tuned them to his note again and given us the right music to play.

An orchestra requires a lot of musicians. We humans aren't the only instruments playing. Think of us as the violins: there are a lot of us, and God has given us the melody line. But there are also flutes and clarinets and trumpets and tubas and bass drums and kettledrums and cymbals—elephants and rhinos and cardinals and vultures and turtles and rabbits and dahlias and lilies and mosquitoes. Every other creature—and even the inanimate parts of creation—is a part of God's choir, is playing in his celestial orchestra. There are no solo parts. We may have to practice on our own, but the real music is played in concert with lots of other musicians.

And it is going to take a lot of practice. Which is why God gave us a group of people to practice with. We call it the church.

6

Ambassadors of Redemption

Madison, Wisconsin, my hometown, is an interesting and fun place to live. It's a great small city, and I love it here—even when the wind chill hovers around forty below. We're regularly awarded "Best Place for . . ." awards by national magazines. In 1996 *Money* magazine thought we were the best place to live in America. In 1997 *Ladies' Home Journal* decided we were the No. 1 Best City for Women; the same year, we were the third-best place to raise a family, according to *Parenting* magazine. And most recently—and appropriately, given the topic of this book—our Saturday Farmers Market, which attracts more than twenty thousand people every week, was rated best in the nation by *EatingWell* magazine (August 2007).

If you're a college student, though, you know about Madison for some other reasons. The University of Wisconsin-Madison was the number-one party school in the country, according to *Sports Illustrated* in 2005. (I hope we've lost the honor since, but I'm not sure.) Students in the Midwest are almost certainly familiar with our annual State Street celebrations—some of us call them riots—on Halloween. Less well known outside the immediate Madison community is a spring rite known simply as the Mifflin Street Block Party. It's a superbly unorganized "event" at which the houses that line four or five blocks of West Mifflin Street open up for "parties"—no further definition needed. It involves hundreds, if not thousands, of people, requires the attention of most of the city police force and costs thousands of dollars in cleanup and related costs.

There's history here. The Party appears to stretch back without a break to the Vietnam protests of 1969. (We may be the only community in the country still protesting the Vietnam War.) The first party began as a peace dance and ended in a riot that lasted three days. And here's a local secret for you: part of Madison's ambivalence toward events like this probably comes from the fact that many of the adults living in Madison today, including those in City Hall and the State Capitol, were students who participated in those early "celebrations."

The annual lead-up to the Mifflin Street Block Party is boringly familiar. As the date approaches, stories in the paper caution about the dangers associated with binge drinking. The university newspaper rehearses the history and debates the city's latest proposals to curb violence and protect the partiers from themselves. This year there will be new strategies and more severe penalties to enforce the rule of law. (We read the same stories last year.) There are letters in the paper pleading for the party to be shut down. (We read the same letters last year too.) In the end, The Party will come. Chaos will reign for a night. Some will be arrested, more than last year or maybe less. Some will be hospitalized. Someone may even die.

And in the morning there will be disaster. Garbage from one end of the street to the other. Partiers will rouse themselves, look at the wreck of the street, and maybe the wreck of their lives. They will wonder, Was it worth it? Eventually city crews will come. The cleanup will begin, and soon the street will be back to normal. Life will go on.

That's the way it has been every year since the Block Party started. But in 2005 something different happened. That year several people from a local church here got a crazy idea: "Let's serve our community by cleaning up after the Block Party." Word went out by e-mail and text message. At 6:00 a.m. on Sunday, more than fifty people, rubber gloves and trash bags in hand, formed a line and began marching down Mifflin Street. In front of them lay a carpet of bottles, cans, paper trash and worse. Behind them, the street was clean. By midmorning, the job was done—but the repercussions were just beginning. Television crews showed up at the church unannounced. The goal had not been publicity, but they came because they couldn't understand what had happened. Why would Christians—opposed to everything that the Block Party represents—get out at six in the morning and do the cleanup? The answer was simple: "We wanted to show what it means to love your neighbor."

This is true Christianity. This is the church at work in the world. When this kind of thing happens, the world notices. It can't help it.

Let the Church Be the Church

This story was newsworthy to the outside world because it was unusual. Who expected a church to do something like that? But it should not have been newsworthy to those of us "inside" the church. Here's an example of a church doing exactly what it was created by God to do. As that line of people formed early on that Sunday morning, they were demonstrating the redemption/reconciliation pattern that I've been describing throughout this book: individuals whose relationship with God had been restored by an experience of forgiveness from God (the first relationship) and who were therefore at peace with themselves (the second relationship) joined hands with other people to work together (the third relationship) to clean up a mess in the world (the fourth relationship). The Mifflin Street Block Party cleanup shows what happens when God's redemptive plan hits the street.

Unfortunately, this kind of initiative remains newsworthy. It's still unusual. And, if we look beyond alcoholic bacchanals to other more common ways in which humanity harms creation, the church is more often to be found among those partying rather than among those trying to clean up the mess. Wendell Berry wrestles with this issue as he considers the effect religion and religious people have had on his own corner of creation through the years:

> Such religion as has been openly practiced in this part of the world has promoted and fed upon a destructive schism between body and soul, Heaven and earth. It has encouraged people to believe that the world is of no importance, and that their only obligation is to submit to certain churchly formulas in order to

get to Heaven. And so the people who might have been expected to care most selflessly for the world have had their minds turned elsewhere—to a pursuit of "salvation" that was really only another form of gluttony and self-love, the desire to perpetuate their lives beyond the life of the world. The Heaven-bent have abused the earth thoughtlessly, by inattention, and their negligence has permitted and encouraged others to abuse it deliberately.[1]

Berry's analysis is perfectly sound. He is describing a Christian experience that sees redemption as applying only to the first or second set of relationships and sometimes to the third. If we can extend our view of redemption to cover all that God intends it to cover—all four relationships restored—Berry's complaint goes away, heaven and earth draw together, and *shalom* becomes more reality than dream.

But what do we mean when we say the word *church*? This is one word that can mean so many things that discussion easily becomes confusing or meaningless. A church can be a building. Or the people who meet in that building. Or a denomination made up of thousands of congregations and millions of people—for example, the Episcopal or Presbyterian or Baptist Church. Keeping in mind that our purpose is to keep things relatively simple and practical, let's avoid theological complexities by employing that useful caveat "for purposes of this discussion."

For purposes of this discussion, we will take it that *church* doesn't mean a building or a denomination. The former never occurs biblically, and the latter is a construct convenient for modern organizational purposes that doesn't have a great deal of application to our discussion. As I'm using the term, there are two interlocking dimensions: Taking a wide-angle view, *church* in the universal sense means the whole Christian "movement"—all of Jesus' followers, moving together, often in fits and starts, but still moving to implement the plan of redemption and reconciliation described in the last chapter. This church might be the worldwide Christian community at one particular time, all Christians in a particular geographical area (the church in Madison, the church in Kenya) or even the entire movement through history, from the time of Jesus to his future return. Changing to a close-up lens, *church* means one group, one subset of the larger group that has joined together in a particular place during a period of time to follow Jesus' teachings, to worship together and to be a community.

Inevitably the meanings will overlap from time to time, for these two dimensions fit together and really can't be separated. The church is always a local fellowship—ordinary people trying to make sense of God's working in their lives and in their community and learning to live and to love each other day by day and week by week. But this fellowship, or these church fellowships, for there are millions of them, always move in an atmosphere that connects them to each other and to those that have gone before and those that will follow—the whole church. The union is almost mystical.

I'm not rambling here! This little excursus is the heart of this book; it's the hinge that connects the great plan of redemption we've been discussing so far with the practical chapters that will follow. If the environmental crisis is a result of our sin, and if God desires, as part of his redemptive plan, that the effects of that crisis be reversed and his creation be restored, this can happen only through the church. Mobilizing the church goes to the very heart of what the church was created to be!

Far as the Curse Is Found

When the church (local) connects with the church (universal), amazing things can and do happen. "Think globally; act locally" describes nothing more than the church of Jesus Christ being and doing what Jesus created it to be and do. The redemption, reconciliation and restoration that God is accomplishing in the world is being accomplished through the church. Cleaning up a street should not be occasional, newsworthy add-ons to a church's program. They should *be* the church's program, as closely tied to the church's reason for being as performing baptisms or celebrating communion.

I've been around the block a few times with the church. I've been a pastor, a deacon, an elder, a youth-group leader, a Sunday-school teacher, a janitor. I even know how to make church coffee (not something one would normally boast about!). I know the church as well as anyone, and I know how far short the *best* church falls from any kind of biblical ideal. There are times when I'm sure that I or anyone could have come up with a better plan than this one.

So why did God go to all this trouble? What was he thinking? Reading the mind of God is presumptuous at best. Granting that, it appears to me that God's plan of reconciliation rests on redemption taking place in the same arena where the curse has reigned supreme—that is, in this physical creation. Isaac Watts put the idea into one of our favorite Christmas carols:

No more let sins and sorrows grow,
Nor thorns infest the ground;
He comes to make His blessings flow
Far as the curse is found.

In God's wisdom, he seems to have decided that the creatures that caused the curse in the first place—you and me, the human race—should be those charged with the job of reversing its effects. It is as if he were saying to us, "You broke it. I'm going to let you help me fix it."

Think about what that means. Unable to earn our salvation or in any way make ourselves right or righteous before God, he has done more than forgive our sins and offer us a restored relationship with him. He is giving us an opportunity to help set right what we caused to go wrong.

Knowing I would shortly be between jobs, an acquaintance invited me to an evening sales demonstration for a multilevel marketing company. We were treated to a review of some very good products—the company makes good stuff—and we were encouraged to sign on as sales representatives; we could earn a commission on each sale to our friends, neighbors or ourselves. But then the presentation got interesting. The secret to success, we were told, was to recruit more people to sell under us. We would get credit for all their sales. And when they recruited more people under them, we would get credit for those sales too. Eventually hundreds of people would be selling, and we could sit back and just rake in the money. This is the essence of multilevel marketing. There are products to sell, but the real goal is to sell memberships. It was quite clear that one of the reasons I'd been invited was because these folks were hoping that I would join so that they could get credit for the sales I would bring in. I didn't join.

Outsiders could be forgiven for confusing some (many?) evangelical churches with multilevel marketing organizations. It sometimes seems as if our mission is to make disciples who will make disciples who will make disciples—until the end comes and Jesus returns to take us all to be with him forever and ever, amen. This is plainly not the case. We ought to reach all nations and see that every person on earth hears the good news of Jesus Christ. Yes! But this is not the end of our mission. It is only the beginning. We broke creation—God is calling us to help him fix it.

So how do we get the mission of the church out onto the environmental Mifflin Streets of the world? How can a group of people who might know how to conduct a prayer meeting but don't know anything about water quality make a difference? What, really, does the church bring to this crisis?

A Values-Based Organization

One of Berry's phrases quoted above sticks in my mind: "The people who might have been expected to care most selflessly for the world have had their minds turned elsewhere."[2] Everyone who wrestles with the problem of Christians and the environment starts at the same point: these people *should* care more than anyone else. Berry's complaint is a pointer to truth: the church has been expected to care and should care about these things more than other people because of *what she already believes.*

My own experience is instructive. When I first began what turned out to be a major shift in career direction toward environmental stewardship, I had to do some intensive self-examination. I discovered something that surprised me: I was already an environmentalist—I just didn't know it yet. I already believed God made the world. I believed he reveals himself through his creation. I believed he put me here to do his will, and doing his will includes taking care of his creation. I had an entire theology—value system, if you prefer—deeply embedded with environmental or creation-care principles. It was packed away in the attic and needed to be dusted off, but it didn't take much to get it out and functioning again.

The same can be said of all of the material I've presented so far in this book. Nothing here is new; if you are a "Bible-believing Christian," you know that everything I've presented is already part of the church's belief system. And I have to say that what has been happening among Christians in this area in the last few years is exciting. If outsiders can figure out that "we ought to care," it shouldn't be that hard for those of us already in the family to figure it out—and then to act on it.

It's time for us to wake up.

A Laboratory for Community

If we are going to successfully respond to the environmental crisis, we—the entire human race—are going to have to learn how to live in community again. Think about how many of the responses to environmental problems have to do with community: community gardens, farmers' markets, car-sharing programs, public transportation systems. They all have to do with living together, working together, traveling together. When we live together in harmony, sharing with each other, buying and selling locally, traveling with other people instead of alone, we make fewer demands on God's creation, and we live healthier—and usually happier—lives.

It should not surprise us that in a creation designed by a God who loves community, patterns of living that emphasize community work better than those that don't. God created human beings out of the community of his eternal trinitarian existence: "Then God said, 'Let us make man in our image, in our likeness'" (Genesis 1:26).

The entire biosphere God produced has community written all over it. Plants can't live without the services of pollinators. Pollinators depend on plants for survival. Even parts of creation that seem at first glance to be in violent opposition to each other—the wolf and the deer, for example—depend on each other. Populations of deer without predators rapidly expand to the point of sickness and starvation, as in much of North America today. Healthy numbers of predators mean healthy deer herds.

And God designed us human beings for community. He made us male and female, anticipating the community of marriage. He placed us in a garden, so as to enable community with himself. All through history, God has been working to form a community. Abraham was chosen not for himself, but to be the father of a great nation. Jesus was raised from the dead as "the firstborn among many brothers" (Romans 8:29). History will culminate gloriously and majestically in what John recorded as "the marriage supper of the Lamb" (Revelation 19:9)— and you can't get much more community-oriented than a wedding.

One of the most important functions of the church now, in this in-between period of history, is to be a demonstration community—to show the world how community is done. Let's face it: community is hard! It's hard in marriage. It's hard in a family. It's difficult in a small town. It's almost impossible in a city. But community is part of how God's creation works, and we'll never live in harmony with creation— that is, we'll never solve the environmental crisis—without learning to live in community again. God designed the church as a community. As a community we have what the world needs if the world is to successfully navigate through the storm of environmental crisis now upon us.

Bill McKibben's latest book, whether he intends it this way or not, is an exposition of this concept. *Deep Economy,* playing on the concept of deep ecology, takes us "deeper" than the balance sheets and profit-and-loss statements that normally encompass what we think of as the economy. McKibben shows us, gently and effectively, that one of the basic assumptions of our modern world—"more is better"—is a fallacy. In fact, once our basic human needs are met, more affluence and increased levels of technology seem to result in a lower quality of life rather than a higher one. And one of the reasons increased affluence results in less happiness and satisfaction is that it almost always comes at the cost of community. We have grown immeasurably wealthier in the last decades yet incalculably more lonely at the same time.

McKibben shows us that the answer to the environmental crisis is the same as the answer to our quality-of-life problem: we need to restore and strengthen our communities. In the pages of *Deep Economy*, he demonstrates one of my own principles over and over: *If it's good for community, it's probably good for the environment,* and its corollary, *If it's good for the environment, it's probably good for community.* As McKibben sees it, one of the answers to the environmental crisis is to regain the kind of community we human beings used to have and which in some parts of the world we still do have.

We've lost community at the same time that we've been sliding toward environmental disaster. Whether this is cause and effect or the two phenomena flowing out of a deeper cause that has given rise to both doesn't really matter. What is important—what McKibben is pointing us to—is that we will not solve the environmental crisis without learning community again. The road back to environmental sanity takes us back to community, from the supermarket to the farmers' market, and maybe from the drive-in church to the old Wednesday-night prayer meeting.

The church is marked by a set of beliefs or values that call her to care for God's creation (among other things). And the church already is what the world needs to learn to be to solve this problem: the church is a community. The church can begin to respond to the environmental crisis simply by being the community she is called to be. (I'll come back to this in the pages ahead, as it deserves exploration.) Obviously a church that gathers to race SUVs through a nature preserve is probably not using the concept of community to advance caring for creation. But for now, it's sufficient to recognize this basic truth: an effective response to the environmental crisis requires that we learn community again—and this is what the church does.

An Agent of Change

As stated in chapter four, the environmental crisis is essentially a disease caused by sin and by sinfulness. Essentially, bad behavior (materialism, greed, selfishness) caused and perpetuated by a tendency toward and an inability to break out of bad behavior patterns lies at the root of the whole problem. Any psychologist or psychiatrist could tell us what we need to do: break the pattern so we can stop the behavior. If this sounds like therapy, you're right. Therapy is what we need. And this is something the church is very, very good at: helping people to understand their sin and guilt, coming to God for forgiveness and help and changing how we live. We need to apply to creation care our ability to confront and change behavior. Environmental problems are sin problems, and sin is something the church knows how to handle.

Will it work? Can Christians make a difference? These are early days, but the signs are promising.

In the Chesapeake Bay area, a community of local fishermen listened to graduate student Susan Drake (now Emmerich) and became aware of the disconnect between what they said they believed in church on Sunday and how they were actually acting when they abused the waters and shellfish beds from which they made a living. They signed a public covenant together—in church—and changed the way they lived and worked in a dramatic fashion. The entire environmental community of Maryland took notice.

In the Pennsylvania farm country, some of those same fishermen took the time to show their Christian brothers that the way the farmers fertilized their fields was damaging the bay and hurting the shellfish beds the fishermen depended on. The farmers determined, before God, that they had to change the way they were farming. How else could they be said to love their neighbors? And they changed.

In Kenya and East Africa, at the conference I described earlier, 260 church leaders signed a public declaration in March 2006, declaring that "we believe that God calls us to be good stewards of His creation" and calling on all Christians in their region to "begin developing God-centered strategies to educate, disciple, and mobilize the entire church to action." A number of churches have since started their own tree nurseries, and plans are being proposed for a Kenya-wide tree-planting effort every year during the week after Easter. The church in Kenya will call the nation to celebrate the resurrection by planting God's trees.

A mobilized church can make an impact.

A Spiritual Organism and a Human Organization

I love my Bible. Not just "the Bible" as a general term, but the particular copy of the Bible that's mine. This copy is getting a bit worn. The leather is seriously frayed on the back, and my wife is starting to talk about how tattered it looks. She wants to get me a new one. She's right, of course, but I'm not quite ready to retire the one I've got. I'm much attached to it, though I could find the same words in a nice new one. The worn pages, even those that have been torn, remind me of experiences I've had with God while reading this book.

That strange mixture of the divine and human is what the Bible is all about. On the one hand, it's a very human document. Written by ordinary people, it was copied by hand for centuries and accumulated copying errors and spelling mistakes. Its thousands of manuscripts and papyri have been the subject of and have stood up under academic research and scrutiny more intense than that given to any other document.

And yet the Bible bears the marks of God's hand as nothing else we possess. It faithfully records history about God's dealings with humanity and teaches about God in language that surpasses any other human literature. Was there ever a poem in any language that could surpass the last half of the eighth chapter of Paul's letter to the Romans for eloquence and passion? Any more universally loved and moving poem than the twenty-third psalm?

And with all this, for millions of us it is an almost direct connection to God. Often I start my day with a cup of coffee and this old, tattered Bible. I read passages that grow more familiar as the years go by, and still I discover new truth. I hear the voice of God's Holy Spirit encouraging or prodding me or in some other way showing me what I need to know today. I don't underline my Bible, but you can still tell which parts have been most meaningful to me over the fifteen years or so that this particular copy has been my mainstay. And that's why I hesitate to give it up. It is a map of a spiritual journey, marking times and ways that God has stepped into my life in a very direct and personal way.

My church is like my Bible, exhibiting the same mix of divine and human. It's a human institution, existing under a charter granted by the secular authorities of my community and my state. It has founding and guiding documents that are legal in character and not very different from those of other nonprofit organizations. It has leaders who are very human and members who are too. It struggles with pragmatic issues like budgets and finances and organizing volunteers and complaints from the neighbors about cars blocking their driveways.

But my church is not just a nonprofit organization. Its human elements are all tangled up with spiritual realities. It's a divine organism as much as a human organization, and there are times when the Spirit is very apparent as he moves among us while we worship and sing praises together. Important actions taken by this church—like buying a new building—have been conducted through the ordinary human medium of taking a vote, but I have no question that that vote was mysteriously guided by the Holy Spirit working through the lives of the people in the room. The divine element in church life is hard to pin down—it defies analysis—but it is nonetheless real. I suspect you might agree with me, and you might also have laughed and cried at the strange combination of joys and frustrations that come from trying to live with the strange organism/organization that is the church of Jesus Christ.

It's this very hybrid character of the church that allows it to bring something unique to the real problems of the environmental crisis. The church can deliver spiritual power to practical problems. The en-

vironmental crisis is a confusing tangle of sinful individual human behaviors, sinful corporate behaviors and the ecological realities caused
by too many people, too many cars, the proliferation of invasive (non-
native) species and the global effects of climate change—and a whole
lot more. It's a scientific problem, an economic problem, a political
problem, a security problem and a moral problem—and a matter of
life and death for millions. But at its root, the environmental crisis is
a spiritual problem. The church—properly understood and functioning in the full power of God—is the only institution or organization
available to the human race that can address a problem with this many
dimensions. The church is capable of addressing every issue: repentance from sin, motivation for individual action, courage and influence to change corporate behavior, and the ability to recruit and mobilize millions of people from volunteers to scientists to move into
creation and do everything from street cleaning to tree planting.

So how do we begin?

PART 2

The Mission
Mobilizing the Church to Care for Creation

7

Like a Mighty Army?

The words ring out bravely:

> Like a mighty army moves the church of God
> Brothers, we are treading where the saints have trod!

But as I look out over this small, Midwestern congregation, it hardly seems like a mighty army. We're in the heart of the American Midwest, in an old farming community. The worshipers are all of European descent. Some have been in this community and in this church for several generations; others are new arrivals. They work their farms and in the local community college and in industry and retail in a slightly larger community west and north of us. They've gathered on this Sunday, as others like them have done here for more than 150 years, to worship, pray, learn from the words of Scripture and wrestle with the issues in their individual lives and their community. When the service is over, their discussions will revolve around the fortunes of the high-school sports teams, the prospect of a cold (or warm) winter and who is going to be on duty for nursery next Sunday.

There is another fellowship, a church meeting on the slopes overlooking Nairobi, in a building nestled among tea plantations. People, ladies in particular, are dressed "smartly" and look like brightly colored flocks of birds coming and going. There are no cars parked at this church; there is no parking lot. Matatus—local taxis that run up and down the road a short distance away—belch clouds of diesel exhaust. There is garbage, especially plastic bags, everywhere you look. The tea bushes, an important source of income for everyone in this church, are withered and dying from a prolonged drought. However, inside the singing is loud and lively. The sermon is prolonged and enthusiastic. The worship service goes on and on and on. When it's over, discussions will revolve around the fortunes of local sports teams, the prospect of rain and who is going to bring the tea for the next service.

The North American congregation is far wealthier than their Kenyan brothers and sisters by almost every measure, but even so, neither of these groups can be considered much of a powerhouse when we think of the challenges represented by the global environmental crisis. They're hardly the "mighty army" of the hymn we were singing that Sunday.

You, my friend, are more likely to be from a church like the Midwestern congregation that I described than the Kenyan fellowship, but I know some of you will come from churches like that as well—in Africa, Latin America and Southeast Asia. Even if you live in North America, more of you are likely to come from a small church than from one of the few megachurches featured in media reports from time to time. We'll have the Saddlebacks and Willow Creeks with us for quite a while, but they will never serve more than a tiny fraction of the Christian community. Most Christians around the world are to be found worshiping in small groups of less than one hundred.

So we can *say* that the church has the ability to address every issue related to the environmental crisis, but it's quite another matter to *see* this actually happening. Perhaps, with the eyes of faith, we can see the church marching through history like that mighty army; when we get down to practical realities, what we actually see is churches—thousands of small groups scattered around the world. Can these tiny groups really be the solution to the greatest crisis facing the human race?

Yes, they can. What appears to be a weakness from a human perspective is not necessarily so when God gets into the picture:

Think of what you were when you were called. Not many of you were wise by human standards; not many were influential; not many were of noble birth. But God chose the foolish things of the world to shame the wise; God chose the weak things of the world to shame the strong. He chose the lowly things of this world and the despised things—and the things that are not—to nullify the things that are, so that no one may boast before him. (1 Corinthians 1:26-29)

God's plans have always been countercultural and counterintuitive. We don't need massive campaigns and buckets of money to apply the solution of redemption and reconciliation to the problems posed by the environmental crisis. We need, rather, to see the church's long-established ability to connect people with God focused on what we have seen is one of God's great concerns: the well-being of his creation.

- We need *worship* that leads us to wonder and awe, that brings us from the beauties of creation to a contemplation of the Creator and from love of the Creator to a passion for the world which he made and loves and wants to redeem.
- We need *teaching and preaching* that builds on this connection, emphasizing the comprehensive nature of God's redemptive plan and our part in it.
- We need to instill these values, this awe and wonder, in *the next generation;* we have to open the eyes of our young people to God's creation—and really, to God himself.
- We need *to reach out to our communities* by not only loving them directly, but also by showing them that we care deeply about the welfare of the world whose Creator we worship and whose mission we're on.
- And, finally, we need to ensure that our *missional outreach programs* integrate creation-care teaching and earth-healing ministry within traditional church planting and evangelism.

Is that all?

Some will scan this list and say there should be a few more items on it. What about political action, for example? It is true that a successful global reversal of the environmental crisis will happen only if there is action at the governmental and intergovernmental levels. Many of the problems can be addressed only by policies and regulations and by incentives and disincentives that must be implemented by government. Should the church not be addressing those who make the policies that go so far to help or hinder progress in responding to this crisis? Yes—but. My concern here is that we in the church have historically been quite good at influencing society at large when we become aware of and concerned enough about a cause. Slavery is one case in point. British statesman and abolitionist William Wilberforce is a legitimate hero both in church history and in the history of the human race. However, from the time of Calvin's Geneva to the present, we have generally not been good at governing. It becomes too easy to be distracted from our primary mission. The church can do the most good for the environmental crisis by simply being the church, as long as "being the church" encompasses the comprehensive redemption that God has in mind.

"Is that all?" can cut the other direction too. This list is a tall order for churches already overcommitted in a hundred different directions. I can hear the groans from the pastor's study. "Another program? I don't think so! No time. No money. Our ministry objectives are set; our strategic agenda has been discussed. If a few people want to do this on the side, it sounds great to me, but don't expect us to drop everything else to pursue an environmental program." I understand the problem. I've spent some time in a pastor's study myself, and I remember the steady stream of pitches by mail, e-mail and phone for this ministry and that ministry. All are valid, and no church can do everything. Each of us, whether at the individual level or at the church fellowship level, has to try to decide what God is calling us to do, and we have to be willing to leave the rest to someone else, even at the risk of leaving some things undone. Some churches will "do AIDS" while others minister to unwed mothers and still others develop food pantries or prison ministries.

Taking this approach, we might expect that "doing creation care" would just be adding to this list of worthy projects; some of us would get involved, while the rest would cheer us on. Um . . . no. There are some powerful reasons why we can't simply put caring for God's creation alongside all other things we might do. Creation care is qualitatively different from other specialty ministries, and it needs to be brought into every aspect of church programming. Here's why.

A Challenge Like No Other

Let's look at the negative first: the nature and magnitude of the problem puts creation care in a category by itself. Nothing—not even AIDS or a flu pandemic in your community—carries the urgency of the environmental crisis.

Let me share a hypothetical story. Let's say that you and I have found ourselves on a ship in the middle of the ocean, transporting a large number of refugees from one country to another. We're part of a Christian relief operation. Crew and staff are in this for reasons of compassion and ministry, and our objective is to care for the hundreds of people on board physically and spiritually until we arrive at our destination.

The needs of the passengers are many. Besides providing daily food and sanitation, there are medical problems, and a host of children to be entertained and educated. We're concerned that the spiritual needs of the people not be overlooked, so we provide opportunities for worship and evangelism as well. To accomplish all this, we've divided our efforts: Some of us provide food and service the restrooms. Others are involved in medical clinics throughout the ship. Still others are engaged daily in caring for children, teaching classes, holding chapel services or just moving through the various parts of the vessel, sharing about Jesus. Some take care of administration, tracking the use of supplies, scheduling use of rooms, seeing that volunteers are used appropriately.

Our voyage proceeds, but sometimes problems appear: an outbreak of dysentery on one of the lower decks, disorganization in one of the kitchens, a disagreement over whether the medical people or the school people have priority for use of a particular lounge. Being sensible folks, we start holding coordination meetings every morning in the captain's quarters to keep track of these issues and to be sure that every service and ministry area has the resources it needs.

One morning there is a new face at the coordination meeting. The captain introduces him: "This is our chief engineer, and he has some news I think you need to hear." It turns out that our vessel began to take on water during the night. The situation is serious, and solving the problem will require cooperation from everyone at the table. "Bottom line, folks? If we don't solve the problem, we can't make it to port."

Think about how that announcement would affect the people sitting around the table. They all have jobs to do; life has to go on, even while the leak is being investigated and fixed. Food still needs to be served. Illnesses still need to be treated. More than ever, people need to be ministered to spiritually. *But the problem with the ship has to be fixed or nothing else will matter.*

This is how we need to view creation care in relation to other church ministries. They all have to go on. No question about that. But if we don't take care of the ship we're on, those other ministries won't matter much. In Haiti, normal ministry of any kind is now impossible due to the terrible conditions in that country, conditions that seem political (violence, kidnappings and so on) but that have their origins in environmental disaster. In countries like Kenya, church leaders recognize their vulnerability. In several informal surveys that we've conducted at Care of Creation, the environmental crisis has ranked higher than the HIV/AIDS crisis in terms of the threat these leaders feel it poses for them and their people. Why? HIV/AIDS *affects* life, but the environment *is* life. When AIDS strikes a community, many people die. When a fishery collapses or agricultural land no longer produces, everyone dies. If the ship springs a leak, everyone goes down. Our earth has no lifeboats.

When Creation Wins, Everyone Wins

There's another, very positive reason for integrating creation care in the church program: becoming more creation-aware and more creation-caring always enhances other ministries in a church far more than it draws resources away from them. This should not surprise us. Extending redemption to all of creation is at the heart of God's plan for the cosmos and the church. The more we "do creation care," the closer we come to actually achieving the reconciliation and restored relationships that are the church's reason for being.

One of the standard objections to environmental initiatives in the political and business worlds has been that it costs too much to be green. Jobs will be lost. We've been told that we have to choose: it's the environment or the economy—we can't have both. Business people are discovering that this is simply wrong. Ford Motor Company recently spent two billion dollars to renovate its flagship Rouge plant in Dearborn, Michigan, and much of the effort went into innovations such as the world's largest living roof (it's covered in a grass-like plant called sedum), the planting of more than 100,000 plants, shrubs and trees and even the installation of three beehives. These efforts are making a cleaner factory for the future, they are reversing some of the damage done in the past, and they are contributing to the company's bottom line. Ford will save millions of dollars a year by going green. Alas, if only Ford had extended that to the cars and trucks it was building, it might be doing better financially. Companies all over the world are discovering that green business—green manufacturing and green products—is good business.

The same is true in your church setting. Green programming will be effective programming. Making a conscious effort to integrate creation care with worship, Christian education, youth programs, facilities management and outreach won't hurt any of these. Every program area will be richer and more meaningful for those who participate, and functional areas like facilities will give back any investment made through thousands of dollars in savings that can be used for ministry activities.

We have nothing to lose and everything to gain. When creation wins, we all do.

8

Creation-Caring Worship

I went to church yesterday. It was a good service. The message was on prayer, and the pastor's text was from the book of Acts. There was nothing specifically connected to God's creation. But three out of the five songs we sang were directly related to God and his world, and the slides used as background for the lyrics were sunsets, mountain landscapes and pictures of galaxies from the Hubble Space Telescope.

Have you noticed that creation has a tendency to sneak into worship even when we aren't looking for it? Check your own worship experience recently. Look at the PowerPoint slides, listen to the words in the hymns or praise songs. Do you see pictures of factories? Of highways and junkyards? Do we sing praise among images of parking lots and shopping malls? Of course not! We see pictures of sunsets and mountains, ocean beaches and starry skies. We sing of nature and creation and the greatness of the God who made it all and who made and loves us too.

It appears that this is because God hard-wired us to respond to him when we experience his world. E. O. Wilson has noted the powerful attraction "nature" has for us as human beings. He's even coined a word: *biophilia*, love of nature. Richard Louv's important work, *Last Child in the Woods*, explores the phenomenon in depth. He shows conclusively that there is something in the human that not only responds to but also needs a connection to the natural world. Children, hospital patients, prison inmates all show remarkable differences when either separated from or connected to creation. Children learn better and show measurably fewer behavioral problems when they have a steady diet of outdoor experiences. Hospital patients who can see nature recover more quickly than those with no view of the outside world. Even prison inmates exhibit different levels of depression and behavioral issues depending on whether they can see God's world or not.

God has designed us to connect with him through creation. And since worship is an activity whose sole purpose is to help us to connect with God, it seems like a logical—even unavoidable—place to begin. Mobilizing the church to respond to the environmental crisis starts with worship. And it's an easy place to start, because most of the work has already been done for us.

Singing and Praying with Creation

Our music, whether traditional or contemporary, is loaded with creation themes. Think about these classic titles and lines of hymns:

- "All Creatures of Our God and King" (1225)
- "Praise God, from Whom All Blessings Flow" (1674)
- "Fairest Lord Jesus, Ruler of all nature . . . " (1677)
- "I sing the mighty power of God that made the mountains rise . . ." (1715)
- "All things bright and beautiful, all creatures great and small . . . " (1848)
- "For the beauty of the earth, for the glory of the skies . . . " (1864)
- "This is my father's world, and to my listening ears / all nature sings and round me rings the music of the spheres." (1901)
- "Field and forest, vale and mountain, flowery meadow, flashing sea / chanting bird and flowing fountain call us to rejoice in thee." (1907)

Note the dates. Not only does this show how well Christian music has aged—many already know most of these hymns that are two, three or even eight centuries old—but it also shows that creation care is not new. Love for God's world and worship that uses God's world is as old as the church itself.

But it isn't just old. Many modern praise songs can also be noted:

- "Shout to the Lord, all the earth, let us sing. / Power and majesty, praise to the King. / Mountains bow down and the seas will roar / At the sound of your Name." (1993)
- "You are the Lord! the Savior of all! / God of Creation, we praise you. / We sing the songs that awaken the dawn." (1994)
- "Lord of all creation, of water, earth and sky . . . " (2000)
- "From the highest of heights / to the depths of the sea / Creation's revealing Your majesty." (2004)

Singing about God's creation is not a modern innovation, but a return to the historical roots of our faith. Throughout history, from David's psalms to today's praise choruses, worshipers and those called to lead others in worship have looked to creation for inspiration—and have found it. Creation-oriented worship upholds some of the oldest biblical teachings we have: "Since the creation of the world God's invisible qualities—his eternal power and divine nature—have been clearly seen, being understood from what has been made" (Romans 1:20). Worship is seeking God's face. What better place to look than in creation?

Creation and worship go together naturally. Worship that leaves out creation is like a piano player using just one hand or a choir that has dispensed with altos and tenors. You can hear the melody, but the richness is gone. Worship that consciously and deliberately incorporates creation is worship to remember and worship that the Spirit of God will use to change people's lives.

What might an effective creation-oriented worship effort look like?

Creation-oriented worship will actively employ creation themes in worship services. I've already shown that this is easy. The content is already there, particularly in music, and it's possible to create a worship service full of creation themes without even trying. But how much richer services will be if we do this deliberately by reading Scriptures about creation as a call to worship, as a bridge between songs or as a transition to a time of pastoral or congregational prayer.

Genesis 1 and 2; Psalms 8, 19, 104 and 148; Job 38–40; Matthew 6:26 and following; Romans 8; and Colossians 1 are just a few of the many passages available. One of the tasks of a worship leader (or worship planner) is to help those who are worshiping to come out of themselves, to leave behind the cares and worries that tangle their souls. Simply drawing our attention to the beauty of the day and making a direct connection to the God who made and rules over the day can do that.

Creation-oriented worship will bring creation into the worship experience. It's unfortunate that the rising influence of technology even in worship has driven us to darken our places of worship (for the use of PowerPoint and other visuals), excluding any hint of the world around us. Worship spaces should make God's world visible! I'll come back to this in the chapter on facilities, but for now, just pull back the window shades if you have windows. You might bring in plants and flowers; during summer and fall, you can decorate the altar or communion table with produce from local gardens. Bring God's beauty in—and talk about it.

Creation-oriented worship will take worship outdoors. Jesus seldom taught in buildings. We see him on mountains, in lakes, walking the fields. Moving the whole church outside seems like a challenge for us, but I'm not sure it would be that hard to do. We might have to learn to worship without technology. So much the better! The church has been worshiping for two thousand years; electronic amplification and air-conditioning are hardly a century old.

It may be time to take a lesson from the classical music folks. In the summer, the Boston Symphony abandons its beautiful (and stuffy) Symphony Hall and heads for the hills. Tanglewood allows musical patrons to experience beautiful music in an exquisite, outdoor setting. I think God is pleased with that kind of combination. Why not try it with worship?

Creation-oriented worship will use creation images in prayer and will bring the power of prayer to bear on the problems of creation. Drawing on images of God's creation will help us to communicate with God in a richer and more effective manner than we otherwise would be able to do. But it's also true that we pray not just to talk to God but also to make requests of him, to ask him to release his power on specific situations in our world. We pray often for healing of our bodies. Sometimes that seems to be almost all we pray about. Why not pray for the healing of our land in a literal sense (see 2 Chronicles 7:14) and for those who are suffering because of environmental causes? Prayer like this will inevitably lead to repentance and confession, and that is as it should be. Repentance and confession taken to heart lay the groundwork for action, and that also is what ought to happen.

Creation-oriented worship will encourage individual worship that incorporates creation. The best group worship experiences lay a foundation for individual worship throughout the week. When we worship together, we model what we will hopefully be doing on our own. Teaching people how to use God's creation in their worship will transform that experience and will begin the process that results in individual behavior and attitude changes in how they live in God's creation.

Preaching and Teaching Creation Care

One of the things I like about our church is that we have really, really good coffee. It's not certain that this church is growing because of the coffee, but it's possible. The service that my wife and I attend is called the Video Café, and it caters to people like me. Sit in the gym on folding chairs and go ahead and sip your coffee during the service. But the coffee service raises an issue: more than eight hundred cups are used and thrown away every Sunday. In a year, that makes forty thousand cups—a lot of waste.

Stony Brook Church in western Massachusetts is different. After-church coffee is just like the fellowship hour in a thousand other churches—but there are no disposable cups. There is a complete selection of real mugs for coffee, tea or hot chocolate. Stony Brook got rid of disposable cups and started using real ones more than five years ago, after a sermon on the implications of Christian environmental stewardship for everyday life. Changing how we use disposable dishes was one of the practical suggestions given, and something must have clicked. Every time I return to this church, I'm pleasantly surprised. The mugs are still there.

This illustrates a couple of things. One is the inherent advantage a smaller church has over a larger one in implementing environmental change. There's no way a church of 2,500 can have a table of mugs available like a small church can. Don't despise your smallness! We don't have to be big to make a difference, and sometimes being smaller means being able to do things a larger church would find impractical or even impossible.

The other thing these mugs are an example of is what can happen when creation-care teaching is a part of worship. There is a mystical power when the Word of God is preached in the context of worship that's not present in a lecture hall or seminar or classroom. When people come together to meet God, when they have spent twenty or thirty or ninety minutes in worship, meditation and prayer, the preaching of the Word has a power that no other kind of speech can match. Political rallies can excite. Classroom lectures can inform. But the Word of the living God, delivered by the power of the Holy Spirit in the context of genuine worship, can change lives.

Lives need to change. At every level, environmental problems are related to individual behavior. Individuals decide whether to buy a compact car or an SUV or perhaps to ride the bus or a bicycle to work. Individuals control home-energy consumption when they turn the thermostat up or down. And individuals make strategic business decisions that impact hundreds of stores or thousands of factory workers. At some point in its development, a new product can be packaged in a way that is environment-friendly or not. Individuals make those decisions.

Here is where the power of the pulpit can make a huge difference, because many of those individuals are in church on Sunday. They should be getting guidance from God's Word as they face the spiritual and moral implications of the decisions they will make in the coming week. The preaching they hear should help them to realize that these are, in fact, moral and spiritual decisions.

Our environmental crisis will not change until people change. And that change will not happen through mailings from the Sierra Club or a platform at a political convention. It will happen when ordinary pastors in ordinary pulpits and ordinary Sunday-school teachers begin to teach about God and creation, and when they help people see the connections between how they live and what is happening to the world God loves.

What should we teach? How about the "full gospel" of redemption and reconciliation already examined in earlier chapters? Incorporating creation themes into worship and prayer will give them a richness they otherwise would lack, and adding creation-care themes—implications and application—to the teaching we're already doing will displace nothing. Instead we'll add a new level of richness, and we'll find new ways to make the faith practical.

Reading Two Books Together

Can we go too far with this? Do we need to worry that an emphasis on creation might lead to a worship of creation itself? Of course. We're humans, given to excess in everything we try to do. We have yet to find a good thing we can't spoil by having too much.

Yes, we might so emphasize the glories of creation that we lose sight of the Creator to whom it points. This would simply be the flip side of the error many of us have committed already: neglecting creation and cutting ourselves off from a whole world of revelation about God. A healthy worship experience will be balanced. It will include songs both about creation and about the Savior. Let's not forget what we already discovered earlier—that one of God's purposes in creation is to reveal himself to us.

He gave us two books about himself: creation and the Bible. We study the Bible with a prayer in our hearts that God will reveal himself to us through the words we read. When we study or meditate on some aspect of God's world, we do the same thing. Whether we see him in a new way in Isaiah 53 or in a spider's web, we rejoice in the vision of the One who made us. When we read both "books" together, it's as if we're cross-referencing the Gospels of Matthew and John. Between the two, a complete picture emerges, and the danger of error is less, rather than more. When we've been in error about God's creation, it has been because of too little time spent in that book, not too much.

9

The Next Generation

No one knows how to multitask like a small-church pastor. In my first church, I did a bit of everything: running the mimeograph machine (this was a *long* time ago), serving communion, planning worship services, preaching sermons Sunday mornings and evenings (a *very* long time ago!) and leading the youth group. Jack-of-all-trades is the title of anyone serving a church of less than one hundred people. Such servants in God's kingdom deserve far more recognition and praise than they will ever find on this earth.

Of all these tasks, my favorite was leading the youth group. Spending time with those junior-high and high-school kids saved my sanity more than once in my five years at that church. We spent a lot of time outdoors together. Annual canoe trips on the Ipswich River north of Boston. Mountain climbing in New Hampshire's White Mountains. Just chucking the day's lesson in favor of a walk through the golf course that bordered our church property. Those "kids"—they are middle-aged adults now—still talk about the time Lisa (a fifteen-year-old from a Catholic family) and I upset our canoe. The rest of the group took great delight in Lisa's impromptu (and very unofficial) "baptism." Some of them have remained friends and are even colleagues in the work of the kingdom almost thirty years later.

I used to think I was cheating when we escaped to the golf course. I had no grand agenda for teaching "creation care." The term didn't exist then. Sometimes it was just easier to go for a walk than to try to keep fifteen energetic and bored teenagers occupied in a stuffy classroom. You know what intrigues me now? I can still remember those experiences, years later. I can remember the mountain. I can remember the canoe trips. I can even recall some of the walks on the golf course. But I recall very little of what went on in the classroom. I wouldn't be surprised if those who were part of the group would find that to be true for them too.

Young people respond to encounters with God's creation, and the effects can last a lifetime. Calvin DeWitt, professor of environmental studies at the University of Wisconsin and founder of Au Sable Institute of Environmental Studies, started his career at the age of three with a turtle in his backyard:

> I grew up right in the city of Grand Rapids, and our lot was only 40 feet wide. But we had a nice home there and my father eventually gave over pretty much all of the backyard to my backyard zoo. And he allowed me to build a special room in the basement for my tropical fish, scorpions, cockroaches, and all sorts of worm cultures that I used to feed my animals. At peak I had 39 parakeets that I was breeding. And I took detailed notes.[1]

Harvard biologist and author E. O. Wilson traces the beginnings of his love for creation to age eight, when his parents gave him a microscope:

> I then found my own little world, completely wild and unconstrained, no plastic, no teacher, no books, no anything predictable. At first I did not know the names of the water-drop denizens or what they were doing. But neither did the pioneer microscopists. Like them I graduated to looking at butterfly scales and other miscellaneous objects. I never thought of what I was doing in such a way, but it was pure science.[2]

Dr. Francis Collins, director of the Human Genome Project, recalls that at age fourteen,

> my eyes were opened to the wonderfully exciting and powerful methods of science. Inspired by a charismatic chemistry teacher

who could write the same information on the blackboard with both hands simultaneously, I discovered for the first time the intense satisfaction of the ordered nature of the universe. The fact that all matter was constructed of atoms and molecules that followed mathematical principles was an unexpected revelation, and the ability to use the tools of science to discover new things about nature struck me at once as something of which I wanted to be a part.[3]

These three prominent men of science have all taken very different paths in life. DeWitt began in a Christian home and has stayed in the faith all his life. Wilson began as a Southern Baptist, but now simply says, "I no longer belong to that faith." Collins traces a journey that began in a free-thinking household and brought him to faith while a young doctor. But they all exude a remarkable passion for God's world. Even Wilson, while admitting that he is a confirmed skeptic when it comes to anything having to do with God, writes almost poetically about God's world:

Without mystery, life shrinks. The completely known is a numbing void to all active minds. Even a laboratory rat seeks the adventure of the maze. So we are drawn to the natural world, aware that it contains structure and complexity and length of history as well, at orders of magnitude greater than anything yet conceived in human imagination. Mysteries solved within it merely uncover more mysteries beyond. For the naturalist every entrance into a wild environment rekindles an excitement that is childlike in spontaneity, often tinged with apprehension—in short, the way life ought to be lived, all the time.[4]

Train a Child in the Way He Should Go

It seems that God's book of creation opens most easily when we are young. But this shouldn't surprise us. Jesus told us that the kingdom of heaven belongs to children (Matthew 19:14) and we might expect that his creation belongs to children in a special way as well.

I referred earlier to Richard Louv's book *Last Child in the Woods*. This is must-reading for anyone involved in Christian education at any level, and most parents would benefit from it as well, particularly parents of children suffering from ADHD (attention-deficit hyperactivity disorder) or anything similar. Today's children are being cut off from nature—from God's creation—and the implications for behavior, inner peace and mature, healthy self-knowledge are frightening and even heartbreaking.

Consider one fifth-grade girl's story:

> I had a place. There was a big waterfall and a creek on one side of it. I'd dug a hole there, and sometimes I'd take a tent back there, or a blanket, and just lie down in the hole, and look up at the trees and sky. Sometimes I'd fall asleep back in there. I just felt free; it was like my place and I could do what I wanted, with nobody to stop me. I used to go down there almost every day. . . .
>
> And then they came and just cut the woods down. It was like they cut down part of me.[5]

I can add to this my own parenting experiences. Animals fascinated our son from his earliest months. By the time he was two, he knew that the Roger Williams Zoo in Providence, Rhode Island, was his favorite place and the center of the universe. The zoo was at that time free, and so we made it a regular outing. He even memorized the route we usually took, past the eagles, stopping by the polar bears, and down past the wolves and so on. I can still remember his favorite route, more than twenty years later. One day, time was short and so I attempted a shortcut. We would skip the wolves this time. My mild son threw a temper tantrum! I can't remember who won the argument, but I do remember how Tim and nature connected so easily. God was speaking to him, even at two years old.

Allowing my children to play in nature has offered me many opportunities to help them to learn important life lessons. One of the many houses we've lived in had a very nice yard that backed onto a wooded hill that sloped steeply upward for about a hundred yards. When our oldest daughter was about four, she loved to climb from the open lawn into the trees that covered the hillside. The slope of the hill was greater than forty-five degrees and it was easy, even for a four-year-old, to climb up. It wasn't so easy to get back down. I still remember the afternoon when I came out into the backyard to find her calling for help. "Help me, Daddy! I can't get down!"

"Well, how did you get up?"

"I climbed (sob)."

"Then climb back down."

"Daddy, I caaan't."

But she did. It took a while, and I was close enough to see that there was no real danger of injury, but the life lesson "You got into the mess, you get yourself out" was learned. Of course, it probably had to be learned again the next week and the week after that and the one after that, but creation gave her an opportunity to test her abilities and to grow in confidence (and maybe wisdom).

We know why children make this powerful connection with creation and why it's such an effective arena for instruction: they've been hardwired by their Creator. Experiencing creation, they experience the presence of God, even though they may not know that's what is happening. If one of our jobs in the church is to help children find God and experience his presence, there's no better way to do this than through the deliberate use of creation in our educational efforts.

The three scientists above—DeWitt, Wilson and Collins—started not only their scientific careers but also their journeys of spiritual awareness in the world of nature, in creation, in God's first book of revelation. And always there were adults—parents and teachers—helping to turn the pages of the book, buying a microscope or letting the back yard become a zoo. But in these stories, and in most stories like them, one seldom sees the church. Let's change that!

Mobilizing the church means bringing the values of creation care to the next generation. As worship is at the heart of what the church is, training and discipleship stands at the center of what the church does. "Train a child in the way he should go" (Proverbs 22:6) is not just for parents. A great deal of church effort and programming is centered, as it ought to be, on conveying the truths of the faith to those who will follow us. We know that we are part of something bigger than ourselves, something that was thousands of years old when we received it and that we are responsible to faithfully pass to those who will come after: "The things you have heard me say in the presence of many witnesses entrust to reliable men who will also be qualified to teach others" (2 Timothy 2:2).

Teaching the next generation is a way of correcting our own mistakes. My generation has neglected creation-care teaching along with creation itself. If that weren't the case, I wouldn't be writing this page right now. Making the effort early to teach values that you and I may have learned late is not hypocrisy—it's love and common sense. Of course, we may find out that our children are already ahead of us and have been waiting for us to catch up.

Teaching a younger generation of Christians to care for creation is one of the things that will help us turn the corner on the environmental crisis for all humanity. The crisis is theoretically solvable. A number of writers are cautiously optimistic that if the right decisions are made within the next few years, the human race can survive. Climate-changing greenhouse gases can be curtailed. The growth of the human population is beginning to slow, and it is now possible to see beyond its peak and to plan for a truly sustainable future. But a lot of work needs to be done, and that work will be done or not done by our children and grandchildren. "Children are the key," says Louv. "What does it mean when Sunday School begins to sound like Ecology 101 and environmentalists (many of them church allergic) begin to sound like street preachers? Good news for both."[6]

Will the children and grandchildren of today's Bible-believing Christians be part of this? I hope so. I hope they will be leading the way and that they will do so because of what they learned in Sunday school rather than in spite of it. What do we need to do?

Leaders Make the Difference

When we talk about Christian ed and youth programs, our minds first go to teaching materials. Is there a curriculum we can use? There is a place for teaching material, but more important than anything else will be having leaders and teachers of young children who understand what God's world is about, who care about it and who can convey that passion to the young people they're teaching.

Your church might have such leaders already. Maybe you're one, and that's why you're reading this book. If not, the best way to start is to go back one chapter. A church that is bringing creation care into worship, preaching and teaching on the adult level will soon have Sunday-school teachers and youth leaders who can do the same thing for young people.

We can't teach what we don't understand. We'll never convey a love for something we don't love ourselves.

Creation Care in Children's Programs

One of the most successful programs at Au Sable Institute is an out-reach to public school children. This innovative program is almost thirty years old that has seen several generations of children from all the surrounding communities come every year from kindergarten through eighth grade for day-long field trips. The program integrates age-specific topics with the state of Michigan's standard science curriculum recommendations for each grade level. Because the children are coming from public schools, the program's teachers do not put Christian content into the lessons. But they don't need to. God's creation has a way of opening minds as nothing else can.

Program director Patricia Fagg explains:

> Within the context of our environmental education program we strive to inspire as well as instruct—to train the heart as well as the head. This type of training is best done through direct experiences in the outdoors. Through the Au Sable program we try to reach each student's imagination, to stir the student's heart

and mind, to awaken enthusiasm, to pique curiosity, and to evoke feeling and action. We try to set the stage so our students will want to know more, will want to discover on their own, and will seek out deeper meanings and understandings.[7]

Patricia is not only a master educator, she's also a scientist in her own right, and she has been doing this for thirty years. Few Sunday-school teachers or youth leaders could match her. But almost anyone can do what she's doing. All you need is children and grass and trees and maybe a pond or stream. It isn't necessary to have a full science curriculum when the goal is creation appreciation, not detailed scientific analysis, although the more science you're able to bring into the discussion, the greater the wonder will be. There's so much to know and learn in creation that it doesn't matter if the teacher doesn't know a lot more than the students; what's needed is a love and an excitement about God's world. Such things are contagious. The students will respond and they will remember. And when the love and excitement about God's world is paired with a love and appreciation for God's Word in a teacher who is able to bring the two together, the result will be an experience that children will take with them the rest of their lives.

My suggestions for incorporating creation themes into children's programs parallel in some ways those in the last chapter for worship.

Take the children out to creation. Get outdoors as often and for as long as possible. God made the sky—he didn't make the ceiling. Go to a park near the church. Explore the stream that borders the property. You can talk about the ducks or you can talk about the old tires, or both. Get an idea of the wonders in the world—find things that are amazing and "cool" and help the kids feel the sadness when that world is damaged, polluted, destroyed. It can be helpful and useful to bring appropriate Bible texts into your discussions, for example, "What do you think Jesus meant when he said, 'Look at the lilies of the field'?" (see Matthew 6:28), or "Did you know the Bible talks about ants?" (see Proverbs 6:6). But don't think you have to have an in-depth Bible study ready every time you go outside with your students. Creation has a pretty clear voice when we let her speak on her own. Really, these will be the easiest classes you've ever taught.

Bring creation in when you can't go out. January in Wisconsin and July in Arizona may not be the best months to spend outdoors with a group of young children. During those times, bring in some unusual pets to show how amazing they are—and how amazing God is. Many of your church members probably have jobs that relate to creation. Pull them in to talk to your kids. Set up an ant farm. Find ways to let creation speak on her own, and your kids will listen.

Instill a sense of environmental responsibility. I'm sure many other parents have had the experience of being a little embarrassed when our younger child spots a person smoking in a public place and says something like, "Ewwww! Daddy, look! He's *smoking!* Isn't that *yucky?*" It happened to us in the 1980s when we were living in Rhode Island, where recycling was a way of life. While our children were in preschool, we went to see friends in the Midwest where—at that time—recycling was unheard of. One of the kids went to toss out a soda can and immediately came running back, yelling, "Mom! They put cans in the *trash* here!" As a child's sense of morality begins to develop, she has a charming way of applying family values with little regard for social tact.

Encourage your students to take environmental values seriously in Sunday school by teaching them to turn off the lights, use a classroom recycling bin and so on. Children who learn that energy waste is a sin when they're six will turn off the lights when they're eighteen. That will take the message home to Mom and Dad much more effectively than any bill insert from the power company.

Encourage further study of creation at the library or at school. An hour a week might whet a young person's appetite, but will hardly satisfy a hungry mind. Convey over and over the idea that God's Word and God's world are like two books with the same theme.

These are little things, and the goal isn't very sophisticated: simple appreciation of God's world. But it's important. Kids who love God's world will grow up to care about it. Those who don't, won't.

Creation Care for Youth

Most youth programs spend plenty of time outdoors. It's a question of survival for the leaders: the amount of energy a group of middle-school or high-school students can generate requires lots of space and plenty of air. So we're out in God's classroom much of the time already. The question is whether we'll make use of that wonderful creation-space or simply do the same things we'd do in a gymnasium. While it isn't a problem to use God's world as a backdrop for a game of Capture the Flag, there are many other opportunities that we don't want to miss.

Let creation speak. A thunderstorm in the middle of a hike, an unexpected encounter with deer, even the sight of a polluted stream or an abandoned car in the middle of "wild nature"—all of these are opportunities to discuss God, creation and humanity. Remember what I've said about creation being a choir. In today's noise-filled world, help your youth learn how to sit still and listen to the birds, the frogs, the wind. Let them also hear all creation groan (see Romans 8:22) by planning a visit to your regional sanitary landfill. This will be a lesson in waste and consumption that the students (and you) will never forget.

Ban iPods and every other device that might block creation's song. Your kids have been immersed in their consumer youth culture for years, and it won't be easy to pull them out of its grasp. But if you can't do it, no one can.

Let the students speak. On a hike, a canoe trip, a quiet evening watching the sunset at the end of a missions trip, when creation speaks, we need to have an opportunity to share with each other what we're hearing. Provide sharing times out under the stars or, if camping, as the sun comes up. These are precious times, especially if you're ministering in an urban or highly structured suburban setting.

Teach creation-care values. "Take nothing but pictures. Leave nothing but footprints." This is a common sign at the start of a nature trail, but your youth will walk right past it. Use the opportunity! Stop your group at the sign, have one of them read it out loud, and talk about why we, of all the other people on the trail, need to heed that sign more than anyone else: "*We* take nothing and *we* leave nothing because *we know the Creator,* and we're taking care of it for him."

Youth programs represent an opportunity to move beyond creation appreciation into the actual care for and healing of creation. You're already doing service projects and missions trips on a regular basis, I'm sure. These can easily be integrated with a creation-care ministry philosophy.

Use service project time for environmental projects. "Adopt a highway" signs are common around the country, and it's nice that groups are making time and effort to clean up our roadsides. I would rather see you "adopt a stream" or "adopt a trail," even if no one gives you a fancy sign as a reward for your work. God didn't make the highway. No matter how much litter you pick up, fish or birds or voles will never be welcome there. Try to go back to the same stream or trail annually or more often, and you'll begin to see your investment in effort pay off.

This will be particularly true if you're able to do ecological restoration work, rather than simply doing cleanup. This might involve removal of invasive, noxious weeds that threaten native plants and animals, or working to restore a native prairie. It's hard work, but your youth have a lot of energy they need to burn. Consistently returning to the same trail, streambed or prairie over five or ten years will develop a sense of history and accomplishment. You can do an Internet search for "environmental volunteer opportunities" in your region or call the Department of Natural Resources or the parks department in your city or county. Volunteers are always needed; volunteer groups that actually show up and then return are almost unheard of.

Include creation-teaching moments on missions trips. If you're going to another country, do some research on the state of that country's environment. Make sure your team members see the damage that's being done to God's creation in that country and how that damage is hurting the people you've come to serve. Learn and then teach how environmental problems make things like HIV/AIDS much, much worse for their victims.

Care of Creation's project in Kenya is located not far from Nairobi, the gateway for many groups coming to serve anywhere in East Africa. A half-day on arrival or departure spent with our staff can give a missions team an excellent perspective on the environmental forces underlying much of the misery and poverty they'll see on their visit. Other countries may have opportunities similar to what we offer, or a local host may be able to find an in-country expert who could give your group the same kind of briefing.

Don't forget the part about wonder and appreciation. Whether in the United States or overseas, be sure that your side trips include opportunities to experience the wonders of God's great open spaces. You'll be amazed how many of the world's biggest/highest/lowest/most unique features you might find yourself near. Find out what geological features are near your ministry site or your travel routes. The deepest cave, the oldest volcanoes, the largest natural spring—all are speaking volumes about God and his world. I wonder how many youth groups through the years have stopped at Niagara Falls and spent most of their time at the concession stands?

Do some career counseling. High-school-age kids in particular are starting to wonder what God wants them to do or to be. As you spend time getting to know each year's batch of youth-group members, don't just look for signs of spiritual gifts. Look for the Calvin DeWitts or the Francis Collinses in your group. Please don't scare them away from science because of fears that they might encounter philosophies or teachings they've never heard before. Rather, encourage them! We desperately need scientists who are Christians, and these might be the very children you are taking on walks right now. With your help, you never know where they might end up. Someday you might be invited to a Nobel Prize ceremony.

Creation Care at Camp

Camping doesn't usually occur in church settings. But camping ministries serve young people (and often adults as well) from local churches. Christian camping and retreat centers are a substantial ministry effort that reach thousands of young people—and many not so young people—every year. You couldn't find a better setting in which to teach about God's creation. The greatest barrier to teaching creation care in any other ministry setting is absent here; with creation all around us, we're already in the classroom. Everything we have to make an effort to achieve back in the Sunday-school classroom is right in front of us.

How effectively are we using this classroom setting? A friend of mine, speaking on this topic at a convention for Christian camping ministries, posed a question for these ministry leaders to consider: "Could you run your program in a gym? If you can, you're not using the resources and advantages God has given you."

How might a camp setting promote creation care?

Bring the background to center stage. Instead of using creation like a set of drapes, make it the main attraction. Set up a program that lets the kids explore the world around them. Use a row of inexpensive microscopes and some jars of pond water. Offer binoculars and bird books. Buy magnifying glasses for examining the bugs under the rocks just outside the cabin door. A program built on creation instead of using it as a backdrop would be easy to teach and would generate its own excitement. Why spend time (and money) making craft projects that will be broken or lost before the summer is over, when we could start a young person on a lifetime of bird watching or plant identification—and teach a lot more about God in the process?

Bring a naturalist on staff. You'll probably want someone with experience teaching kids in the outdoors who has a biology, environmental science or other natural science degree. Our Christian colleges produce many such graduates every year, and some would just love to spend their summers showing kids the wonders of bugs. Talented undergraduates could serve as nature counselors as well. Undergraduates obviously won't stay around, but a partnership with Au Sable Institute or a Christian college could provide a steady stream of young and enthusiastic staff members to whet the appetites of your campers.

Build your Bible teaching programs around creation care. At the risk of sounding repetitive, the world and the Word belong together. Select Bible themes that speak to God's concern for his world—such as those in the first half of this book—or ones that can be illustrated from the natural world. A series on Jesus' parables, for example, could be very effective in an outdoor setting. That, after all, is where Jesus was when he told most of these stories for the first time. Try illustrating the parable of the mustard seed while sitting under a pine tree two hundred feet high, holding a quarter-inch pine seed. Worship and study of the written Word helps us understand and interpret the created world, but wonder and appreciation of God's creation also throws light on the written Word.

Find out who's doing interesting things in creation near your camp, and incorporate them into your program. Take the campers to visit the fish hatchery or an organic farm (or even a not-so-organic one). Make a field trip out of cleaning trails in the local state park. Ask a local environmental official to help you with an inventory of your camp property. You might find important restoration projects that could be started in your own backyard. These would help your own land to become more like God originally intended it to be, and it would probably help the land of your neighbors as well. Such projects are usually labor intensive, but you have a camp full of young people who have energy to spare. Teach your campers that caring for God's creation is both important and fun.

Incorporate creation care in facility management and food service. Compost your waste. When you have to build or landscape, use the best techniques available. Be energy conscious. Use camper labor to rid your land of exotic weeds. Eat low on the food chain—more vegetables, less meat. And let your campers and their parents know that caring for God's creation is one of your organization's core values. You might be surprised at the response you get, and you might find that a well-advertised "green Christian camping" program will attract parents and children who aren't interested in church, but who do care about God's world. In business, "green business" is good business. In the competitive world of camping, "green camping" is a good ministry strategy.

Creation Care on Campus

Over the past thirty years, the environmental studies landscape at Christian colleges has changed dramatically. At the beginning of that time, no Christian colleges offered majors in environmental science. Few offered courses in it, and there were no full-time faculty in this field. Today fifty-seven Christian colleges are affiliated with Au Sable Institute of Environmental Studies. Many of these offer an environmental science or environmental studies major and have dedicated faculty. Several of the larger schools have their own field stations.

Environmental activities at these colleges go beyond the classroom. A number of schools—Gordon and Messiah, for example—have active, campus-wide recycling programs. Gordon successfully recycles 35 percent of its waste and estimates that using efficient lighting fixtures saves the college more than twenty thousand dollars per year.[8] Messiah's figures are similar. Goshen College in Indiana boasts Merry Lea Environmental Education Center, a 1,150-acre preserve that features one of the very few LEED (Leadership in Energy and Environmental Design) Platinum buildings in the country and that serves seven thousand local elementary school students and teachers each year.

Unfortunately, Gordon, Messiah, Goshen and a few other Christian colleges are the exception, not the norm. At many other schools, environmental science faculty members are struggling, often alone, to bring the message of creation care to the mainstream of college life. This isn't surprising, since campuses reflect the attitudes and priorities of the churches from which the students come, but it has to change. Colleges and seminaries have often led the rest of the evangelical community and can do so again.

The scientists have done their part. We know from them what the problems are, and we have a good handle on some of the solutions that can be deployed. But scientists won't fix the environment. It will be fixed by business leaders, politicians and pastors. Especially by pastors. Few people will exert more influence for good or for ill than the leaders of tomorrow's congregations. And we know exactly where these future leaders are: they're in class right now, in Bible college and seminary. They're studying Greek and Hebrew and homiletics and systematic theology and counseling and youth ministry and . . . almost everything but environmental theology or creation care.

We need Christian colleges and seminaries to review their programs in light of the need to mobilize the church for this crisis. This could begin with regular chapel programs and hosted conferences, but should ultimately require every future pastor to have a course in creation-care theology. The students in class today will influence the entire church community—and our nation and world—toward or away from a healthy attitude about God's creation and an adequate response to the environmental crisis.

The opportunity for the church to bring creation care to campus is not limited to Christian colleges. Christian student groups on secular campuses have a unique challenge and opportunity. The challenge lies in the fact that much of the secular world is well ahead of the Christian community both in awareness of the environmental crisis and in taking action in this regard. But that doesn't mean we can't join in! This book has largely been about the unique perspectives and abilities the church can bring to the environmental movement. All of this is also true of the microcosm represented by a Christian student group on campus.

A student group's opportunity is in the fact that creation care is a largely untapped resource for sharing our faith with others. Try setting up an outreach table and asking people their opinion about the environmental crisis. Introducing ourselves to the campus community as Christians who care about God's creation is likely to get lots of questions and some positive public notice. Taking this further with service projects like those described above (cleanup, restoration and so on) will reinforce our verbal message of love with a practical demonstration.

There are some indications that a student-based Christian environmental movement may be beginning. An A Rocha chapter at Wheaton
College (you can find them on the arocha.org website) is a couple of
years old and is hoping not only to mobilize for change on their campus, but also to see groups established on campuses across the country.

The environmental crisis took a long time to reach the critical stage
we now face. It will take a long time—much more than a generation—
to bring creation and civilization into harmony again. It's our children—that next generation—that will see this through to a successful
(or otherwise) conclusion. Let's help them start now, and let's do it as
the church.

10

Godly and Green

There are reasons the church I attend is growing explosively: The teaching is good. The pastoral staff is hard working and dedicated. It's a fun and vibrant place to worship and connect with other Christians. We have what many would consider a good problem, but it's still a problem, as the pastor will be happy to tell you: too many people are showing up for worship. The facility was designed for about five hundred people—and more than three thousand now attend nine services from 8:00 a.m. to 7:00 p.m. every Sunday. Parking was a challenge, and relationships with the neighbors were understandably frayed. Would you want to live across a narrow street from a church packing in that many people? In spite of the best efforts of an army of volunteers and repeated announcements in church, God's people were blocking driveways, creating muddy ruts on the edges of the road and making life difficult for our neighbors.

What's a church to do? Moving appeared to be the only answer; you can't stop people from coming, even if you wanted to. The mission of the church in general and this church in particular calls for an open door and an invitation that is as physical as it is spiritual. So our church has moved. Several months ago we moved into a brand new building well outside the current development boundaries of our sprawling city. What was pasture and cornfield last year is now a muddy building site, and shortly will be the new home of Blackhawk Church.

Please understand: I am not questioning the decision to build or where the new building is or even how it was built. A variety of other options were considered before making the final decision. A site was selected in careful coordination with city authorities, who already had plans for the development of the new area. City and church worked together to implement a number of the principles of new urbanism, including sharing parking facilities with neighboring businesses. And the building itself incorporates a variety of principles advocated by the LEED (Leadership in Energy and Environmental Design) rating system, though the cost prevented full LEED certification. I don't know that I would have done anything differently.

But still. Another farm has been ploughed under for suburban buildings and a parking garage. Most people will have to drive further than they did to go to church, unless they move into some of the several thousand new houses going up in the same neighborhood in the next couple of years. It isn't any easier to put creation-care principles into practice at church than it is at home or at work. Whether your church is growing into a new building as we are or rattling around in a 150-year-old mausoleum, it isn't easy being green.

Mobilizing the church means applying creation-care principles in the siting, design and operation of our church buildings and grounds. It's manifestly true that "the building is not the church—the people are," but the facilities that house a congregation are important. Like your own physical body, they're the visible, public face of the church. Church facilities that squander energy or that are surrounded by acres of parking and lawns soaked in chemical poisons are an embarrassment to the glory and reputation of the God they represent. It's not easy to bring our church facilities into line with what we're learning about creation-care principles. But we have to try. Some things can be done.

Planting Is Greener Than Building

Church planting is a viable environmental strategy that will become more important as energy prices continue to rise. Anyone planning a new facility should count on the price of gasoline (to drive to church) and natural gas, electricity and heating oil doubling every ten years from here on out. In ten or twenty years, it may not be possible for people to drive thirty minutes or an hour to a large church facility on the edge of town. The biggest consumption of energy in a large church is probably the fuel used by the cars used to get there; one of the biggest challenges to church attendance in the next twenty-five years will unquestionably be the cost of driving.

Big churches today tend to follow a shopping-mall model: large facilities that draw from a very large area. In a future marked by high transportation costs, the McDonald's model may turn out to be a necessity: smaller, neighborhood-based facilities to which people can walk or drive a short distance. Wouldn't it be great if the church, rather than reacting ten years late to developments in society, were to anticipate those developments by planting small, efficient, friendly neighborhood churches? Planting is always greener than building.

Designing for Worship

As I approached the church where I was scheduled to speak, I knew I'd seldom seen one in a prettier setting. Built on a hill overlooking a highway, it was nestled against a patch of trees. Standing outside the front door, I could see beautiful Wisconsin countryside for miles on three sides. But when I entered the sanctuary, all the beauty disappeared. Moderate in size, seating maybe two hundred people, it was of fairly recent construction and had narrow windows on one side. All the windows were covered with blinds. You got just a hint that the sun was shining, but no more. It didn't matter what the weather was like— it could have been a cloudy, rainy day, or it could have been snowing in August—we would not have known. God's world was completely shut out from our worship.

Then there's Lake Edge Lutheran Church in Madison. The lake in the church's name is Lake Monona—pretty enough, but a block and a half and a very wide avenue away from the church. Buildings, parking lots and traffic surround the church itself. There seem to be far fewer opportunities here to create a creation-filled worship experience than at the church described above. Not so. The sanctuary had been built with windows and lots of wood and stone, giving worship a bright, airy, natural feel. Pastor Dick Blomker recently shared with me and showed me how the congregation had updated the rest of the forty-year-old building (increasing the useable floor space by 40 percent while reducing utility costs by almost as much) and created worship spaces and fellowship areas that emphasize natural lighting and connections to the congregation's past.

I know why more churches look like the first example than the second. PowerPoint slides project better when the windows are shaded. There are less distractions, we think, when we can't see the world outside, so we can focus better on the worship service. And it's probably cheaper to build a big, dark barn than to go through all that Lake Edge Lutheran went through to achieve what they did. All of this may be true, but think for a minute of what we're losing. Imagine your feelings if you walked into a church and the greeter at the door took a look at the Bible in your hands and said, "Welcome to our church! In order to avoid distractions during the message, we'd like to ask you to leave your Bible here. You can collect it again when you leave." Absurd. Illogical. How could having a Bible distract me from worship? But that's what we do when we design worship spaces that shut out God's creation. We're cutting ourselves off from that "other book."

Let's bring creation back into the worship area. Let's design with natural light and with windows so we can see God's sky and experience his weather and respond to the changes of the seasons as the year progresses. Such a setting can enhance the worship experience in unexpected ways. Some years ago I was preaching in a community church that was meeting at the time in a Catholic monastery. The chapel we used had windows set high in the south wall in such a way that the sun could shine into the middle of the hall. It was a cloudy day, but just as I reached a particularly emphatic point in the message, the clouds broke and the sun burst through as if God himself was saying, "Listen up! This is important!" The congregation seemed to get the message. Worship spaces designed for total human control of lighting and sound tend to remove God's Spirit from the equation. We're the poorer for it.

Following are some suggestions for designing or renovating worship spaces that will allow God's creation to have a voice in worship:

- *If you are building, select a site—or the worship space on your site—to allow views of creation instead of human-made structures.* One of the most important principles of environmental design is providing natural lighting sources, because it saves energy. The great thing about this is that it works two ways: if the light can get in, we can look out. Pay attention to how the sun will come in during your primary worship hours. Careful design will still allow for darkness when needed.

- *Even if you're in a mostly urban or suburban setting, it doesn't take much land to set up a screen.* Plant trees, shrubbery and flowers between the windows of the sanctuary and the parking area or mall next door. Put out some birdfeeders and get the young people involved in maintaining them. You might find Psalm 84:3 happening while you watch.

- *Incorporate elements of creation in the interior design.* Natural wood, stone, fabrics that bring out the colors in nature—all will contribute to your worship experience in a deep, almost subliminal way. And let's not go the plastic plant route. Plants, yes! But plastic? Plastic plants are to real ones what paper plates are to fine china.

Similar principles can be applied to rooms other than the sanctuary, of course, such as fellowship areas, lobbies and classrooms. Make it so that everyone who enters the building sees the connection between God and his world. And don't forget to make that connection clear in the worship and teaching that goes on there.

Lead with LEED

If you are building—if you must build—become familiar with the LEED program. Leadership in Energy and Environmental Design, sponsored by the U.S. Green Building Council (www.usgbc.org) is a comprehensive, point-based certification program to encourage new construction and renovation projects that are appropriate and based on the best current green thinking. LEED certification is expensive; levels range from Certified through Platinum, and points are awarded for every aspect of construction, from site preparation and disposal of building materials to energy conservation and sourcing of the materials used in construction. A LEED-certified church building would be a powerful statement to a community that "this congregation cares." Even if you can't afford full certification, get your building committee and contractor to study the principles and to see how many you can implement.

As of this writing, LEED is mostly oriented toward commercial office structures, which is certainly applicable if you're constructing a large, suburban church building. However, they are in the process of developing a LEED for Schools program that will probably be applicable to churches.

Being Energy Stewards

Lake Edge Lutheran, mentioned above, has managed to increase square footage while decreasing utility costs phenomenally. Also consider the Reverend Charles Morris and the St. Elizabeth Catholic Church in Wyandotte, Michigan, who found their way into the pages of the *New York Times* recently. If you visit this suburb of Detroit, you can find the church by looking for the windmill and the solar panels on the roof, the front porch and the garage. According to the *Times,* Father Morris reduced his congregation's annual energy bills by more than twenty thousand dollars per year. He says, "We're all part of God's creation. If someone like me doesn't speak about its care, who will? The changes we've made here, that's a form of preaching."[1]

Energy use is a moral issue. We're entering a period of global energy scarcity as indicated by the rapid increase in the world cost of oil. Occasional "declines" in oil prices, when they occur, simply emphasize the point. Not many years ago, a rise to current levels would have been shocking. Energy prices are driven by one thing: demand. As painful as the cost of energy may be for you and me, it's much more painful for our brothers and sisters in other, poorer parts of the world.

Every unit of energy we use we buy in competition with other users who have much less than we do. Our demand drives the price of their energy up, as well as our own. Minimizing the use of energy in our church buildings as well as in our vehicles and homes is a moral issue because every unit of energy we use is taken from someone else who needs it as much or more than we do, and every unit we save is available for others to use.

Use of energy from fossil fuels is also the major driving force behind global climate change. Every puff of greenhouse gas that your church pumps into the atmosphere adds to the problems being caused by climate change, increasing future damage on God's creation for your children, your grandchildren, and your Christian brothers and sisters around the world. It's simple to help. All we have to do is reduce the amount of energy we're using. At the same time, we can check with our local utility to see if it's possible to purchase "green power" from sources like wind. Many utilities now offer this as an option.

There are few better places to demonstrate stewardship and "loving our neighbors" than in how we operate our church facilities. Most church buildings are big. They use a lot of energy: heat in the winter, electricity for air-conditioning in the summer, lighting all year long. We purchase commercial chemicals for cleaning and flush the residue into the water system. The opportunities are clear, and the benefits are substantial. It costs nothing to be good stewards; it's almost always an effort that results in substantial monetary savings.

- *Heat and air-conditioning.* Get a professional review, and make the investment needed to update your systems. Computerized building controls and new high-efficiency HVAC units will almost always pay for themselves quickly. Even if savings seem marginal right now, don't forget the moral dimension.

- *Building insulation.* Keep the energy you've already expended inside. Enough said.

- *Lighting.* I hope you've already switched from incandescent to long-life fluorescent bulbs. Great progress has been made in lighting technology in the past few years. And use common sense! I was in a church sanctuary that had large windows and plenty of natural light coming in, but all the interior lights were still on.

- *Office machines.* Turn them off at night. Be sure all your computers are set to shut off the monitor after fifteen minutes and hard disks after thirty. If you turn off the power strip itself, you'll eliminate the "phantom load" from standby power. A 10-percent reduction in energy use is almost guaranteed. (Your machines will last longer too.)

- *Cleaning supplies.* It might take a bit of research on the Web to find green cleaning supplies, but the effort will be worth it. If you're a church custodian, your work is important, and this is an area where you can put some effort and care into your job and make a substantial contribution to the creation-care ministry of your church. Speaking of green supplies, stay away from soaps that advertise themselves as antibacterial. These antibiotic soaps do more to encourage the growth of resistant bacteria than almost anything else.

- *Reusable cups, mugs, dishes and so on.* One easy way to switch to reusables is this: get people to bring their own. It would be an unusual commuter who doesn't have a travel mug that she uses all week long. Why not on Sunday as well? Not very many years ago, standard church dinner procedure was "bring a dish to share, and bring your own dishes to eat from." One church encourages this practice by letting everyone with their own dishes go to the front of the line. Bringing dishes helps to eliminate work in the church kitchen, saves the cost of disposable dishes and cuts back on a lot of waste. Why send God's money out the back door in trash bags to mess up his world?

Glorifying God on the Grounds

The grounds that our church buildings sit on should be places where God's creation is celebrated. But if your church is typical, your church property is comprised of parking lots, lawns, landscaping shrubbery and not much else. Nothing grows on a parking lot, and the green areas are probably soaked in chemical poisons to keep the grass green and to kill everything that wants to compete with it—plant, animal or insect. Is this really the best return on investment for the Owner of the property?

None of us intend to do harm to God's creatures when we set out to have attractive landscaping that fits in with the suburban culture that surrounds many of our church buildings. We want to enhance the reputation and ministry of the church. But when we manage church property just like everyone else, we become part of the problem. Our lawn chemicals are silently destroying God's worship choir while we're inside singing,

> All things bright and beautiful,
> All creatures great and small,
> All things wise and wonderful,
> The Lord God made them all.

A church surrounded by nothing but parking lots and suburban grass is squandering an opportunity to bring glory to God by creating a place for God's creatures to live, a place that could then be used by people who are looking for God in his world. It doesn't take a lot of space to create a patch of trees and shrubbery that can be homes for birds, squirrels, rabbits and many other wonderful creeping and crawling things. Your church property might already have some pockets of leftover creation—corners of the property you haven't "developed" yet. Or you could bring in trees and plants. Put in walkways and benches. Make an outdoor classroom that classes or youth groups can use regularly. Learn to chase out the exotic weeds and bring in the kinds of native plants that God designed for your neighborhood. And invite your neighbors to come and enjoy God's good earth with you. You might even find that some of them enjoy your outdoor worship space so much they decide to see what's goes on inside.

Let me tell you about my friend Paul. The retention pond at the large suburban church he attended was just plain ugly. Required by the city to help control storm water runoff, it looked like a huge storm drain in front of the property. It had been neglected while the new building was being built and had even received some unwanted building materials from the church construction and from other houses being built in the neighborhood. It added nothing to the attractiveness of the church grounds, and to some like Paul, it was an embarrassment.

Paul had done restoration work on his own rural property, and he was a member of a local prairie restoration group. He discovered that there was a temporary gap in church oversight—no one was in charge of that part of the grounds—so he gathered a group of people and got to work. He enlisted some church members who were landscapers and a person with connections to the city parks department who was able to secure prairie plants. They cleaned that area and planted it with native plants. Today that ignored and ugly piece of land is charming and beautiful and full of flowers, birds and wildlife. It's the most attractive part of the church grounds, and recently became something more for the congregation: a memorial garden where church members remember loved ones with the donation of a tree or shrub, marked by a boulder carved with a favorite Bible verse.

A huge eyesore has become a center for the life of the congregation.

Here are some quick suggestions to help your church grounds glorify God:

Develop a multiple-use management plan for your church grounds. At most of our churches, the grounds are a giant welcome mat leading to the front door and not much more. This is a waste. Parking is necessary, but it may be one of the less important contributions your property can make to advance the mission of the church. Go back to the sections on worship and education, and look at your church property again as a potential extension of those ministries.

Minimize artificial landscaping (like lawns) and maximize natural areas. These are just as attractive, less expensive to maintain and will give God's creatures places to live. In Wisconsin, prairies are popular because they're native to our region. In your area, it might be a patch of New England hardwood forest or a cactus garden. Landscaping experts in your community would love to help and may even donate services; some of them might be in your congregation. If we put back what God used to have here, God's creatures will come back on their own. We just need to give them a chance.

Where you have to have lawns and parking, use materials and methods that will do the least damage to the soil and creatures. Lawns can be managed without chemicals. Check <www.safelawns.org> for ideas and suggestions. Improvements in parking-lot technology include porous pavement—materials that allow rainwater to soak through into the ground, and *grasscrete*—cement tiles with spaces for grass and plants to grow through, but with the strength to support vehicles. This might be a very desirable option for a facility that only needs to park large numbers of cars occasionally. The rest of the time, your "parking lot" can be grass.

Plant your church's history with a memorial garden. We encourage congregations to develop a "tree-planting culture." Designate space for people to plant trees or shrubs, and start making it a family habit. When a couple gets married, have them plant a tree. When babies are born, plant a tree. When people leave this earth for heaven, plant a tree to mark the occasion. A master plan and a list of desired types of trees can guide individual families. "We have room for ten fruit trees on the west side. Would you like to plant a cherry tree in memory of your dad?" Within a decade, even a small congregation could have a substantial, beautiful and very meaningful church forest. Just imagine a young couple having their wedding pictures taken under a tree planted by the bride's parents when she was born. That is the kind of richness that creation care can add to the life of a congregation.

Bring Creation to an Inner-City Church Setting

I was encouraging a group of pastors with some of the suggestions I mentioned here. One man raised his hand and asked, "When I look out of my church's windows, all I see is a parking lot and a gas station. Is that what you have in mind?" His urban church was meeting in a storefront. He had plenty of windows already, but the view outside was nothing that would bring glory to God or enhance worship.

No one needs a touch of God's creation more than those who are living, working and worshiping in the city. Urban church settings offer unique challenges, but if you live in the city, you'll already have noticed that creation dies hard. Every sidewalk, empty lot and polluted stream shows plants struggling to live and to sing praises to the Creator. As long as we're in the city as well, let's try to help them grow by giving them space.

Every urban situation is going to be different, but here are some thoughts to get you started:

Try to make creation visible from your worship space. Windows to let in light can be shielded from the gas station or graffiti with a screen of plants outside, inside or both. You might want to put a bit more effort into some plant life inside the worship area as a contrast to the concrete jungle outside.

Adopt an empty lot nearby for a community garden. I know of few church-sponsored community gardens, though Boise Vineyard has a good example of one. It is hard to think of a more effective way to blend caring for creation with caring for the community in which we live. If people are poor enough to need a food pantry, they can certainly be blessed by an opportunity to grow their own food. (I'll touch on this again later.)

Adopt a park or stream and get your youth group or Sunday-school classes to tend it. Don't just "clean it up." That's a one-time effort and usually not very satisfactory. Adopting implies going back over and over again, and seeing the accumulated results of your efforts, which is much more satisfying. Refer to the section on children and youth for ideas on how to incorporate such activities into your church program.

The building and grounds are not the church, but they are the part that the community sees. They are small parts of the great worship space called creation. What we do with them matters; it can make all the difference in how we and those around us learn to see God in his world and to care for that world.

11

Loving Our Communities

Pastor Tri Robinson followed his convictions and finally preached a sermon on environmental stewardship at his church in Boise, Idaho. He admits that he was terrified. But he also knew that one sermon by itself would mean nothing. If this truth—that God's people have to care for God's earth—was important, it had to become a visible reality in people's lives. And it did.

Before he preached that sermon, Tri laid the groundwork for a church-based recycling program. His staff researched local volunteer opportunities to present to the congregation. Now huge recycling bins line one side of the Boise Vineyard parking lot. "Tithe your trash" brings in hundreds of pounds of recyclables every week. Recycling containers are prominent throughout the church campus. Teams of church volunteers regularly arrive at nearby National Park Service trailheads to maintain trails, plant trees and assist the park service in caring for some of the wilderness areas with which Idaho is blessed. The church's outreach to victims of Hurricane Katrina was funded in part by an effort to collect and recycle cell phones throughout the city, a program that resulted in a number of community members arriving at the church on Sunday morning to find out what this green congregation was all about.

Pray (and Work) for the Peace of Our Communities
We have already seen that integrating creation care and worship is important and necessary for our own sake and that of our children. Creation-caring worship is richer; creation-caring education is more

effective; creation-caring facilities enhance ministry and save money. And of course, caring for creation is the ultimate goal of God's redemptive plan and therefore the main reason the church has for being the church.

But all of this has another important effect as well: when creation is hurting, people suffer. Healing creation is one of the most meaningful, practical and long-lasting ways we can love our neighbors. This is probably most obvious when we think of missions and the way in which people in developing countries are suffering from the effects of environmental degradation. In our next chapter we'll examine that issue. However, let's be clear: the effects and costs of the environmental crisis are not limited to the slums of Nairobi or the eroded hillsides of Haiti. Our own communities are suffering. Though the causes are often hidden and the effects are in some cases only beginning to be visible, they are nonetheless real.

Just as "missions begins at home," creation care begins in our own communities. We who are God's people have a responsibility to these communities. The prophet Jeremiah's words to the exiled Jews in Babylon remain true for us today:

> Build houses and settle down; plant gardens and eat what they produce. Marry and have sons and daughters; find wives for your sons and give your daughters in marriage, so that they too may have sons and daughters. Increase in number there; do not decrease. *Also, seek the peace and prosperity of the city to which I have carried you into exile. Pray to the* LORD *for it, because if it prospers, you too will prosper.* (Jeremiah 29:5-7, emphasis added)

In an environmental sense, we Christians have perhaps spent too much time singing, "This world is not my home, I'm just-a-passing through," when we should have been following Jeremiah's instructions to "seek the peace and prosperity" of the cities where we are temporary residents. We have a world that has been damaged, and we have to be involved in the healing process.

My Corner of God's Creation

Madison is far from an environmental basket case. We have been the recipient of quite a number of quality-of-life awards. We are blessed with a state government that has a strong interest in protecting forests and wildlife. But even here, trouble is not far beneath the surface.

After thinking for years that we had some of the best water in the country, we've recently learned we don't. There are contamination problems in a number of our wells, and aquifers that were supposed to last a thousand years are already beginning to decline.

All our lakes suffer from the overfertilization of suburban lawns and are being overrun by a variety of exotic plant and animal species, including Eurasian water milfoil and the infamous zebra mussel. A scary fish disease called viral hemorrhagic fever is only one or two watersheds away from infecting our lakes and prize trout streams.

A noxious weed called garlic mustard overruns our woodland, and mature trees throughout the state are in danger from a tiny insect called the Ash borer. Acid rain threatens, though most of "our" acid rain falls in Michigan.

Farmland throughout the area is being swallowed by housing developments and big-box retail development. Farmland that is still in production is more often than not the source of enormous amounts of chemical pollution, and CAFOs—the euphemistic label for "concentrated animal feeding operations"—are proliferating, accompanied by air and toxic waste problems never before encountered in these rural regions.

We're running one of the dirtiest power plants in Wisconsin just three blocks from the Wisconsin Capitol building, and in a state with some of the best sport fishing in the country, we're warned about eating fish from our rivers and lakes because of mercury poisoning from the same kinds of power plants.

None of this compares with the body blows creation is taking in Kenya, Haiti and many other countries, but these are still wounds to God's world. As a member of Christ's church, I bear a responsibility for what is happening to his creation here. There's not much I can do to solve some of these problems in Madison, but I can do something.

A list of environmental problems in your community will be different. It might be longer than Madison's, but I'd be very surprised if it was
any shorter. Think of it this way: We are God's people in _____
[insert the name of your town]. This is our corner of God's creation.
What are we doing to take care of it?

So, what *can* we do?

Just Being the Church

One of the most effective ways that a church can be involved in responding to the environmental crisis in its own community is simple:
just be the church. Because environmental problems are sin problems,
an effective response to an environmental crisis requires a change of
attitude and a change of behavior toward God's creation, growing out
of a change of heart that only God can produce. In other words, we
can start to respond to the environmental crisis by reaching people
with a message of love and forgiveness, and by getting them into
church. However, this will work only if we're getting them into a
church that preaches and practices the kind of full-redemption caring
for all of God's creation that I've been talking about here.

When I speak about these topics, I'll sometimes have with me a
cloth shopping bag full of goodies to illustrate some of the things I'm
talking about. One of these is a container of heavy plastic that I
bought at my local drug store. It holds about half an ounce of dry pancake mix and is designed to make cooking pancakes as easy as possible. You just add water up to the line along the top, shake, pour into
a hot skillet and voila! You have two (or maybe three) fresh, hot pancakes. You'll have paid approximately five times the cost of ordinary
pancake mix, and the weight of the plastic packaging, which consumed energy and petroleum to produce and will never be used again,
weighs three times as much as the pancakes themselves. This kind of
product is an obscenity, the very existence of which indicates the reasons for our environmental crisis.

But here's my point: That product passed through a number of stages of development, from the first person who came up with the idea to numerous meetings of committees and task forces to determine what the packaging would look like and how it would be priced and marketed. If the people involved in development were members of a church where they were learning of their responsibility to care for creation *even in the decisions they make at work*—well, I might not have had to write the paragraph above. Every product and every policy that contributes to the environmental crisis has human fingerprints all over it. A church that's doing its job in terms of evangelism, discipleship and creation-caring, full-redemption teaching will be shaping the decisions more effectively than any store boycott or petition to Congress could do.

Yet many aspects of this problem—land-use policies, tax incentives or disincentives, crop subsidies, fuel-economy standards and so on— can be handled only by government. Should a church provide leadership or opportunities for action at this level? I'm not sure there's one answer to that question. On the one hand, the environmental crisis is a moral crisis just as worthy of the church's attention as the problem of slavery in the days of William Wilberforce two hundred years ago. On the other hand, we in the church have not always been successful when we've dabbled in politics even for worthy causes.

One of the things we need to keep in mind is that honest and sincere people can agree on a goal and disagree significantly on how to reach that goal. Renewable energy is something few people would not want to see. But what kind of renewables should we promote, and how will we get there? Price controls? Tax incentives? Others? The harmony of the body of Christ—the church—is a precious thing, and wise congregational leaders and pastors will take care that the goal of caring for God's creation is not lost in the heat of argument over what may be secondary issues.

Get Your Hands Dirty

Many of the suggestions for children's and youth programs will directly benefit your corner of God's creation and provide a bridge of outreach to your community. These don't have to be limited to young people—everyone in the church can be involved! Projects that have a direct impact on the ecological health of your community will make a difference in what your town looks like, how healthy your neighbors (and your children) are and how your community views your church, especially when such projects are continued year after year after year.

Generally, creation-care activities can fall into three categories:

1. Creation appreciation. We need to spend time learning about what we want to save. Whether it's the creatures in the woodland that borders a city park or the birds that visit on their annual pilgrimages north or south, few of us know or appreciate much about God's world. What we don't know, we can't appreciate. What we don't appreciate, we won't care about. What we don't care about, we won't try to fix or to save. Many of the activities discussed previously—outdoor worship services, Sunday-school classes and youth group meetings, nature walks, stream adoption—will accomplish this goal. But similar events could be planned for and with the rest of your community.

Earth Day comes every April, often close to Easter. Our society has tended to co-opt many originally religious celebrations and festivals for its own purposes. Think "Easter" and "bunnies," and you get the idea. There's no reason we can't do the same thing in the other direction. Rather than ignoring Earth Day as a quasi-pagan spring rite, as some do, we should be grabbing the concept and using it to celebrate God's creation at the same time we're celebrating Christ's resurrection. There are some themes here that run together, you know.

2. Creation healing. Many things can be done in every community to bring healing and restoration on a practical level. Almost all of them require little skill but a lot of people, which is perfect for churches, because generally we're good at jobs that take people power. Pulling noxious weeds like garlic mustard, cleaning trash from stream beds, planting trees or prairie plants, and clearing and maintaining hiking trails are all examples of ways that the man-, woman- and child-power of your congregation can make a meaningful contribution to the health of your corner of God's creation.

One of the most healing things that can be done to a piece of God's creation is to use it to grow food. Most home gardening done with a reasonable eye to good practices like composting and minimal use of chemicals will be a blessing to the soil and to the creatures who live there. It's possible to garden in such a way that the land becomes more fertile and productive every year rather than less so. I'd like to see a congregation encouraging its people to garden, turning over a part of its property for use as a community garden and then finding ways to get all that food into the hands of those in the community who need it. Communities that garden tend to have more food than they know what to do with at harvest time. In some places, the only time you need to lock your car is in September, to keep your neighbors from filling it up with tomatoes and zucchini. Now think. There are hungry people in your town; there are in every town. Those empty fields behind your church—you know, where the new education wing is supposed to be built one of these years—you can use that land. You can heal the land and feed the hungry at the same time.

3. *Lifestyle transformation.* Many of the larger problems in creation—energy use, climate change and the negative effects of consumerism—can be solved only by changing the way we live. We have to change our individual behavior, from the frequency with which we replace our iPods to the kinds of cars we drive and the number we own. Much of this will come from an effective and informed teaching and preaching program that emphasizes the kinds of values that creation-caring Christians should be exhibiting in their lives. But it will also come from a healthy community life within the congregation. Changing is easier when we do it together. Churches can encourage appropriate lifestyle changes in a variety of ways: promote carpooling and the use of public transport, sponsor "bike to church" days, collect specialized items for recycling that public programs won't handle, like batteries, cell phones and printer ink cartridges. Incidentally, cell phones and cartridges can be sold for a nice source of income for one of your church missions projects or youth programs.

Such activities will generate returns on a number of levels. Church members who go out and spend a Saturday working with each other will get to know each other. They'll meet people who would otherwise never enter a church building, and they'll have a basis for conversation that can lead on to genuine friendships. And a part of God's creation will be healthier and more as he intended it to be.

Caring for God's creation is something that many members of our communities care deeply about, even when they don't know or believe in God. Environmental matters affect the common good of all of us. When a church professes to love its neighbors but doesn't care about the water or trees, those neighbors can hardly be criticized for questioning the sincerity of that love. Ignoring creation-care issues results in a deep disconnect that undermines efforts to reach our communities.

A church active in caring for all of creation will be appreciated and will find genuine and increasing respect for its message of eternal redemption. Activities that heal creation—and even better, that lead in community-wide creation-care efforts—will bring people into the church that otherwise would never enter the door. Many of those who are involved in environmental stewardship projects at the local level are young, idealistic and passionate. They need meaning in their lives, something to do and something to love, and they've found it in a passion for God's creation—even though they don't know that's what it is. They are without deep philosophical (or theological, if you like) reasons for what they're doing, but they know things are going badly in nature and they want to fix them. They're easily discouraged because the problems are too big; the powers that be are distant and daunting. People like this have half a foot inside the door to God's kingdom already. Imagine a gospel message that connects their instinctive care for God's creation with his eternal work of redemption through Jesus Christ.

Build a Community

As I go back and forth on my errands in Madison, I occasionally encounter a car parked in one of the city garages with a sign on it: Community Car. Shared vehicles is one answer to the problem of transportation in a crowded city and an energy-starved world. One car serves many families, the opposite of the usual suburban situation where the number of cars in the driveway is sometimes greater than the number of people living in the house. Car sharing is good for the community and good for the environment.

Similarly, near the center of Madison we have the Willy Street Co-op—a full-service food cooperative that through the years has grown into a full-service market. The food is good, fresh and organic. Anyone can be a member. It's good for the community and good for the environment.

I've had trouble counting the number of farmers' markets going on in Madison this summer. We have the big one downtown every Saturday morning—twenty thousand people packed in so tightly they can walk only in one direction around Capitol Square. But there are at least half a dozen others on different days of the week. Good food, good prices—and talk about community! Last week I bought vegetables from two different booths: one run by a family who has been farming the same land for 160 years, the other by a Hmong family that has been in Wisconsin just fifteen years. They were side by side. Farmers' markets—good for the community and good for the environment.

Do you see a pattern here? Authors like Bill McKibben are showing us that responding to the environmental crisis is going to require that the human race learn to live in community again. Much that we see in our modern world, from private automobiles to iPods, serves to undermine or destroy community. The path back to environmental sanity seems to lead back to community.

What is the church, if not a community? The church is committed by her charter to be a community—the people of God. As the human race faces the greatest crisis in its history, the solution appears to lie in learning to live in community again. This is not a coincidence. The church is in a place where all she has to do is be herself and she'll be doing what is most needed to solve the environmental crisis.

Green Evangelism

We have to be careful about how we tie creation care into our evangelism efforts. Letting our friends and neighbors see us as people who love and care for God's world can give us a powerful bridge to relationships. Sharing such a fundamental value can—and often does—become a platform for sharing many other things, including our love for Jesus and our desire that others would learn to love him too.

But green evangelism can also become a tool for manipulating people. I've made a case that God's redemptive plan is intimately connected not only to his love for the human race but also to his love for the rest of his creation. This has to mean that anything we do that helps to heal creation—whether recycling plastic bags, reducing energy consumption or restoring a degraded stream—is worth doing on its own merits. We don't do these things in order to "lead people to Christ" or as a means to increase the attendance at our church. Taking that approach sounds, and is, just a bit hypocritical, and if there's one thing that many secular environmentalists are very good at, it's sniffing out hypocrisy.

Having said all of that, there is no question that a vigorous and visible creation-care program will go a long way toward enhancing and enriching any evangelistic outreach program you already have, just as it will enrich worship and improve children's programs. That's because this is what the church is supposed to be doing, and doing it will improve everything else your church is trying to do. But it's also true because non-Christian environmentalists are people with strong values, at least in this area. Take note of this: they care deeply about something God also cares deeply about. They're more than halfway to a relationship with God already, no matter how cynical about "religion" they may appear to be.

Two things jump out at me here. First, on the positive side, one of the great challenges in sharing God's love with people is overcoming their preconceived ideas about him. How much easier when we can let people know that the God we worship loves his world as much as they do—more, in fact—and that he's the one who put that love for the world in them in the first place.

Second, on the negative side, consider the great damage done when a person who loves God's creation but doesn't know him encounters a Christian who says he knows and loves God but shows by his words or actions that he really doesn't care much for God's creation.

As with every other aspect of church life, an outreach program that incorporates caring for God's creation will be richer, more effective and more in tune with God's ultimate desires for us as his people. It's only a small step from community outreach to missions—our effort to share the gospel and the love of Jesus around the world. That's where we'll go next.

12

A Healing Mission

Not long after we started Care of Creation as an environmental missions organization, I sat down for coffee with an old friend, the retired principal of the missionary school that both my wife and I attended as children. He's a man who played a key role in my early life and for whom I continue to have great respect. As I shared with him the concept behind Care of Creation, environmental missions, loving people by helping them to heal their part of God's creation and so on, I could tell that I was stretching his ministry and theological categories almost to the breaking point. We weren't exactly on the same page. He finally put down his cup of coffee, looked me in the eye and said, "Ed, what in the world does this have to do with the Great Commission?"

If you've stayed with me this long, you have a pretty good idea of why I believe caring for God's creation has everything to do with that final command that Jesus gave his disciples: "Go and make disciples of all nations" (Matthew 28:19). I've made a case for full, creation-caring, creation-restoring redemption. But my friend's question is a serious one. He has seen the primary message of the gospel of Jesus Christ diluted by various kinds of "social gospel," and he believes he has some reasons to be nervous. Is this just one more effort to make a timeless gospel relevant, focusing on human needs but cutting out the essential heart of redemption and forgiveness of sins through Jesus' sacrifice on the cross? The history of Christian ministry is littered with the carcasses of organizations that attempted to adapt to the needs of the moment and in the process lost the spiritual power that made them unique.

So how is caring for creation different? The first part of the answer requires a review of the theological foundations laid in the first part of this book. Christian missions is the effort of the whole church to extend Christ's ministry of reconciliation (see 2 Corinthians 5:11-21) to all nations and all peoples, making disciples and "teaching them to observe" all of Jesus' teachings and commandments (Matthew 28:20), in effect teaching them to live in ways that will reverse the curse of sin throughout all of God's creation.

We've seen that this process involves a restoration of each of the relationships broken at the time of Adam and Eve's sin: our relationship with God is restored in *salvation*; our relationship with ourselves in *sanctification*; our relationship with each other in *koinonia*, the restored community of the church; and our relationship with nonhuman creation in learning to live in harmony with it again, a process reflected in the ancient Hebrew word *shalom*. (See chapter five for discussion of these themes.) If, then, the purpose of Christian missions or ministry is the accomplishment of this kind of full redemption, including creation care is not a distraction from the main goal. It is the goal.

Countries like Kenya have experienced more than one hundred years of missionary presence, but their current state shows no improvement. Depending on what you want to measure, Kenya is possibly a great deal worse off than before the gospel arrived. Is there a correlation between this and the truncated view of Christian missions we've promoted for the last century? If the biblical goal is *shalom*, but we thought we were finished when we delivered a simple message of *salvation*, it's no wonder things haven't worked out quite as well as we might have expected. Bad theology—or at least incomplete theology—will always give bad results.

Jesus warned his disciples of the dangers of casting out a demon and leaving the "house" swept, cleaned but unguarded. That demon returns with seven others more powerful than itself (see Luke 11:24-25). We have driven out the demons of paganism with a lightweight gospel of personal salvation. Today the churches in these countries are reaping the harvest. If we're honest, the results of this are evident not just in the daughter churches of missionary-receiving countries, but also in many of the mother churches that sent missionaries out in the first place. Bringing creation care and missions together will restore the theological integrity of the missionary enterprise.

There is a more immediate, though perhaps no more important, reason for paying attention to this issue. Environmental degradation is reaching the point where we are in danger of losing much of what has been accomplished over this last hundred years. Consider Haiti. Close to the North American mainland, Haiti has been a favored destination for short-term missions trips, youth group teams and extensive development and church-planting efforts. Hundreds of organizations and thousands of individual Christians have taken part in efforts to reach and serve Haiti. Few countries in the world have enjoyed greater attention from North American Christian missions than this small island nation.

In spite of all that effort, Haiti remains one of the saddest countries on earth. Packed with people, wracked with violence, afflicted by successive governments, each of which exceeds its predecessor in incompetence and corruption, Haiti represents one of the worst cases of environmental collapse in the modern world. Ninety-seven percent of its forest has been cut down. Agricultural land is washing into the sea. Tropical storms that kill dozens on neighboring islands kill hundreds and thousands on Haiti. Without forests and their soil, there's nothing to absorb the rainfall, so flash floods and mudslides are the rule. Jared Diamond sums Haiti up in one sentence: "The question that all visitors to Haiti ask themselves is whether there is any hope for the country, and the usual answer is 'no.'"[1]

In all of this, missions work in Haiti has practically ground to a halt. The security situation is such that missions trips are no longer possible, and most missionary efforts have been sharply curtailed and or have ceased because of the danger to staff.

Kenya, where Care of Creation is at work, is not as desperate as Haiti—at least not yet. But many of the same elements are at work. Rapid population growth, serious deforestation, decline of agricultural productivity due to erosion and loss of fertility on the remaining land means that today a greater percentage of the population lives below the poverty line than when missionaries first arrived. The missionary effort has been "successful"—the churches are full of enthusiastic worshipers—but the land is hurting, the people are suffering, and it doesn't take much imagination to see a Kenya ten or fifteen years from now that looks much like Haiti does today.

I know these are complicated situations. There are a lot of factors at work, including the failure or absence of economic, government and environmental policies. I can't help but wonder, though, if a more complete gospel at the beginning—one that taught the kind of respect for God's creation discussed throughout this book—might have helped. When a country is 80 percent Christian, as Kenya is, those running the government are almost certainly products of Christian families, churches and even schools. Is it unreasonable to think that a different approach to God and his creation throughout might have resulted in different and more effective government policies?

However we arrived at this point, we're here now, and we face a critical five or ten years ahead. Kenya, Tanzania, Uganda, the Philippines—all are approaching environmental and ecological tipping points. Like Haiti, these countries could dissolve in political turmoil that makes ministry almost impossible. Or they could pull back from the edge and have stable and even prosperous futures. Which direction Kenya, for example, turns will depend very much on Kenya herself. But the Kenyan *people* will drive Kenya as a nation in one direction or the other, and the church in Kenya is perhaps the most important institution in determining what the choices will be. It bears a heavy responsibility here, as the church in North America or Europe does to its own country. However, to the extent that the Kenyan church is tied to Western missions or development organizations, these Western entities have an important role to play in helping to respond to the environmental crisis.

There is one more reason for including creation care in our missions programs: we are commanded to love our brothers and sisters, and more and more this means helping them to cope with degraded environments. James warned his readers against expressing pious thoughts while ignoring practical needs: "Suppose a brother or sister is without clothes and daily food. If one of you says to him, 'Go, I wish you well; keep warm and well fed,' but does nothing about his physical needs, what good is it?" (2:15-16).

Whether the reasons people are without clothes or daily food are environmental, economic or political, we have no choice—we must respond out of love for our brothers and sisters and out of obedience to the Word of God. Mobilizing the church means responding to the environmental crises in other countries as an act of love toward brothers and sisters in Jesus. In churches in North America and other countries that send missions workers, we need to become aware of the reality of the international environmental crises and include environmental ministries—like Care of Creation, Floresta and A Rocha—in our missions budgets. Christian environmental projects need to be funded and expanded. There is a lot of work to be done and not much time if we are to avoid more Haitis in the near future. Equally important, missions agencies and Christian organizations of all kinds need to adapt their outreach and development strategies to include creation-care teaching and projects. Remember my ship story: if the ship goes down, all the other programs go down with it.

What if we were to establish a new model of missions that would set out both to reach people and to bring Jesus' redemption and reconciliation to the land, air, water and all of God's creatures? What would that look like? Following are ideas designed for organizations working on these problems. I hope that some of you "back home" will review these as well and consider how you can encourage the missions workers and the organizations you already support to aim their efforts in this direction.

Theologically Sound

First, we have to be sure that creation-care missions efforts, like any other kind, are theologically sound. That is, we have to ensure that our missionary theology includes everything we've been talking about in this book. Bad or incomplete theology leads to bad results, but good theology will result in comprehensive, holistic approaches to missions outreach efforts.

Sound theology will keep bringing us back to the root causes of the problems we face. It's easy to get so focused on the practical challenges of tree planting, for example, that we lose sight of the sin problems we're also dealing with. Environmental problems are sin problems, but they don't present themselves that way. Erosion on a farm may be the result of sinful neglect, but that's not apparent. What we see is muddy fields washing away. Deforested hillsides need to be addressed with boots and gloves. Diseases caused by environmental pollution need clinics and new government policies. Practical concerns and issues tend to make themselves into priorities, so it's easy to create programs that leave theology at the door.

What is called for is a practical theology, or praxis—theology in action, as it were. Our Care of Creation staff work hard to integrate theology throughout our projects: "Farming God's Way," "Planting God's Trees" and "Harvesting God's Water" are more than slogans. We use such language to remind participants and staff alike that everything we do is related to God and his original creative designs for this earth.

An emphasis on sound theology will encourage a central role for the church in every country. "Mobilizing the church" means just that, whether the church in question is in Boston or Nairobi, Boise or Manila. Modern missiology recognizes that planting churches means accepting those churches as full partners in the work of the kingdom. We'll want to be sure that our model for creation-care missions places the responsibility for God's creation where it belongs—on the shoulders of each local church body. The church in Kenya will answer to God for the condition of his creation in her corner of the world. We Christians in Madison will answer for what we've done to ours. We can and should help each other, and this shared responsibility is an acknowledgment that the church is key to responding to the environmental crisis in each place. A theologically sound program will focus on empowering and equipping the church to respond to whatever environmental challenges are evident in its particular area.

What does "theologically sound" mean in practice?

- *It means creating strategies and plans that are biblically based.* Because it's easy to leave theology at the door, we have to be intentional about it. The power of the church comes from our beliefs and our reliance on God day by day. It can't be lip service.

- *It means working through local church structures.* In every setting, the church that God has placed there is the party whom God has entrusted with the care of his creation. All of our projects and efforts have to be designed to strengthen and help the local church to be what God wants it to be.

- *It means developing staff teams that know why they're doing what they do and that are constantly reminded of the underlying theological principles.* Training in technical subjects should be paired with appropriate biblical teaching, both on the job and in regular refresher training courses.

- *It means relying on prayer as much as planning.* Sometimes you just have to go out and clean a streambed. But including both private and group prayer before, during and after a project will help us keep the streambed project going smoothly—and will be a strong reminder of why we're doing what we're doing.

Scientifically Informed

Good theology is vitally important, but theologians are probably not the best people to tell us what kind of trees to plant. We have to be careful that our efforts are scientifically informed. God has given us a complex world, and mistakes are easy to make and hard to fix. Take the eucalyptus tree. Fast growing, adaptable and with commercially valuable wood, it seemed like the answer to Kenya's deforestation problem. Hundreds of square miles of eucalyptus were planted.

Another success story, yes? Not quite. It turns out that this tree, designed by God for its native Australia, wasn't as ideal for Africa as it first appeared. For one thing, the eucalyptus is a thirsty tree. In a dry climate, where every drop of water counts, a grove of eucalyptus acts like a giant pump, sucking water out of the soil and away from all the trees and plants around it. An African sister told me recently, "If your neighbor has a eucalyptus tree, forget it. Your own farm will be dry."

Then it turned out that African insects didn't like eucalyptus. The fragrant oils that Australian animals like the koala love drive African bugs away. While this would not seem to be a problem to me and to you, it's a big problem for birds that eat bugs. With no native insects, African birds can't live in eucalyptus groves. A God-designed ecosystem has plants, animals, birds and insects that know each other, need each other and live well together. A system that tries to combine Australian trees with African bugs and birds just doesn't work. As eucalyptus has spread, habitat for birds has decreased and water problems have increased.

Some mistakes are reversible, and this is one. A number of years ago, Brackenhurst International Conference Center, where our Kenya project is based, began removing eucalyptus trees and replacing them with indigenous varieties. Almost immediately the birdwatchers in the area noticed a difference. Before the project began, a survey found thirty species of local birds on the grounds of the center. That number is tragically low for Kenya, which claims to have 1,089 native bird species, more than any other country. Recently, just a few years after the eucalyptus were replaced with bird-friendly African trees, a visiting couple counted 140 species.

Here are a few suggestions to be sure that a missions project is scientifically informed:

Use people with appropriate environmental or scientific backgrounds throughout the project process. Scientifically qualified advice doesn't have to be expensive. One of the virtues of scientists is that they're often looking for places to test their ideas, and sometimes they have money or can write grants to get it. I know of several college professors who have spent a number of years traveling to various parts of the world to share their expertise. This benefits not only those of us working in those countries but also the professors, who are able to bring real-world experience back to their students. Hosting a professor for a semester or year-long sabbatical is a way to gain top-level advice at very little cost. You may find that you have access to international nongovernmental organizations or intergovernmental organizations like the United Nations Environmental Program (UNEP) in your area, which would be pleased to partner with you. Your successful project makes them look good too.

Establish a planning, implementing and review cycle that helps you to know what's really going on in your project area. This means allowing enough time at the front end to ensure that you really understand the needs of the area; going in without predetermined ideas as to what the project is going to be about; and ruthlessly evaluating every aspect of the project to see if the short- and long-term goals you wanted to achieve were actually met. The planning process is key, but review is an equally important phase often overlooked in the missions world.

Avoid donor-driven project goals. Donors (and even board members) sometimes have pet project ideas that may not be what's needed in a given situation. During the Pakistan earthquake recovery, my staff and I came across a straw-bale house being constructed by a major international relief organization. Straw-bale construction is an innovative technique appropriate in some parts of the world, but not in northern Pakistan. We were intrigued, so we stopped to ask about the project. It turned out that the organization had a wealthy donor who was convinced that straw bale is the answer to everything, and so they were building a straw-bale house to please him.

This happens more often than we want to admit. The customer may always be right in retail, but the donor is not always right in missions. Approach your donor with solid technical and scientific reasons for your proposed project; reputable donors will appreciate your prep work and so will the project recipients.

Develop student-internship or research-sponsoring programs. These are opportunities to benefit from the presence of someone who has studied the latest material, while giving them the chance to apply and test that material. Internships are normally taken by students in the upper levels of undergraduate work or between undergrad and grad programs. Research would be conducted by master's or Ph.D. candidate students.

Geographically Comprehensive and Politically Savvy

Many missions efforts and environmental projects are local in focus and scale. One village or one neighborhood or perhaps a group of villages is targeted for evangelism or relief efforts. Some projects, like tree planting or watershed restoration, work effectively at this level, since local people are affected by the problems and can be involved in remediation efforts. Many environmental problems, however, do not respect community boundaries or national borders, so geographically comprehensive strategies are needed.

For example, consider a current set of problems in Kenya. In overcrowded slums in cities like Nairobi, people need fuel to cook their food. They buy charcoal from street vendors because there's no other fuel available. Their demand for charcoal drives deforestation deep in the hills, miles from the city, as equally poor people sneak into national forest reserves, sometimes bribing government officials who often are as poor as those bribing them, to cut down trees and burn them into charcoal. These activities in turn devastate farmland miles away and far down the slopes from the forest where the trees were actually removed. Without the forest, the farmers' water source becomes erratic, swinging from drought to flood and back again. The farmers also contribute to the problem by collecting wood for their own use or for charcoal.

Care of Creation's strategy in such a situation is to help these farmers to manage their land carefully and in accordance with biblical and scientific principles. We've found that farmers are eager to learn and want to do everything they can to preserve what land they have left. But as long as the trees continue to be cut on the slopes above their land, the farmers are fighting a losing battle. The government officials who manage the forest, and who also are probably Christians, need to learn to care for the forest with a new sincerity. The woodcutters, very likely Christians as well, need to understand that their method of making a living is harming God's creation. But they'll need help, such as another source of wood for charcoal or another means of making a living. No matter what, the residents of the Nairobi slum will still need fuel, so some alternative source might need to be found.

How can we create projects that address needs comprehensively rather than piecemeal?

Do your scientific homework first. Good preliminary research and surveys should uncover the links between local problems and problems in other areas. Bring in some of the professors and grad students mentioned above to do a research project for you. The problems are complex, and easy solutions will be tempting. Don't fall into a eucalyptus trap!

Establish regional partnerships with other organizations and regional government offices. If organization A is doing reforestation upstream and organization B is working on erosion control for farmers downstream in the same watershed, a great deal of synergy can result from regular consultations and active partnerships. In the case of Care of Creation's work in Kenya, we're seeking to encourage churches and schools over a wide area to establish nurseries and to develop their own tree-planting programs. Some of those churches are in areas where other development organizations are at work, and it's helpful for both them and us when we let each other know what we're doing.

Encourage churches and denominations to establish their own regional or national partnerships. Care of Creation's biannual God and Creation conferences have begun to create such networks in the Christian community in Kenya. We'd like to see such conferences held in neighboring countries as well, and eventually throughout the African continent and beyond. Blending Bible teaching with practical workshops, such conferences result in effective training, increased enthusiasm and a healthy network of relationships among churches across the conference area.

Problems like these can't be solved without becoming involved in political and economic realities. Aggressive and affirmative government action is sometimes the only way forward. While political involvement is not the role of a missions organization, it is the legitimate role of the church in each country. Church members, ordinary Christians whom God has placed in positions of influence, can create and enforce policies to preserve God's creation. They will understand—because of teaching from their pastors and because of their own convictions—that this is what Christians do. Others will enforce the rules they've been sent to enforce as government officials for the same reason: their faith tells them to be faithful in this task. Farmers and city dwellers alike will make small, daily decisions to live simply and to walk the earth softly, because they've been taught that this is the same earth Jesus walked on and that the redemption that means so much in their own lives also has meaning for the birds, animals and trees.

What in the world does caring for God's creation have to do with missions? Everything, my friend. Everything. This is how a mobilized church can change the world.

13

And Finally

On October 8, 2005, a devastating earthquake shook the northern mountains of Pakistan. Seventy-six thousand people died. Thousands more sustained serious injury. Hundreds of thousands of homes were destroyed. Around the world, millions of people watched, listened and responded to the crisis. I arrived in Islamabad at 7:00 a.m. on November 8, one month after the quake. By 8:00 a.m. that same day, I found myself sitting at an enormous conference table with forty or fifty people representing a few of the many organizations engaged in a massive relief effort. Some represented government or large non-profit organizations and were clearly professional "disaster fighters." Others, like me, had been called in from other duties and occupations for a month or longer to do what needed to be done. The sense of urgency was apparent. Winter was coming, and the possibility was real that initial disaster could be compounded by thousands more deaths in the five to ten feet of snow that could be expected.

The effort to beat the winter emergency was called Project Winter Race. And it succeeded. Tents, emergency shelters, blankets, stoves and food were distributed by the ton. Strategies were tried and failed. Organizations adapted, and other attempts seemed to work better. Convoys of trucks and jeeps and an international fleet of helicopters ferried supplies to the most remote locations. One United Nations official called this one of the most complicated but best-run disaster recovery operations he had ever seen.

There were hundreds of organizations involved, but the heroes were not the organizations. The heroes of the Pakistan earthquake were ordinary people who made extraordinary efforts. A doctor from Sweden served beside another from Korea. A group of eighty Cuban doctors, who could speak neither English nor Urdu but who communicated love and compassion for people, drew praise from all sides. Construction workers from California, who had heard that help was needed building emergency shelters, gave up vacation time and paid for their own travel. And many ordinary Pakistanis gave time and money to help their people during a time of need.

When disasters occur, it is people who make the difference. Organizations are just tools. They help us to coordinate and work together, but their effectiveness (or lack thereof) is in the individuals who sit behind the desks, answer the phones and drive the trucks. In this book I've been talking about *mobilizing the church to respond to the environmental crisis.* But in the end, *the church* can't respond. Only individual Christians like you and me can do that. We should work together in and through our church families to involve others and to multiply our efforts. But my church will remain on the sidelines until someone in that church decides to do something. So will yours. Some of us could legitimately say that we're "just ordinary folks," while others have positions of considerable influence and responsibilities for leadership. But all of us have a personal responsibility to do what we can wherever we are right now.

May I address my final words to some specific people in the church?

Dear Pastor,
In the introduction I referred to biologist E. O. Wilson's book *The Creation,* which is a letter to a pastor. Wilson recognized two things: religion—the church—is influential in society, and pastors are influential within the church. Those of us who are or have been pastors may chuckle at that; we know how little influence we really have at times. But I'm not sure that the good professor is entirely wrong, though he might not understand why or how he's right.

What I'm thinking of is the unique power of preaching. The

preaching of the Word remains a sacramental act; it's not the same as a lecture at the university, and it packs more punch than a movie distributed nationwide. It's an awesome and sacred duty that carries potential for influence far greater than many of us who practice it realize. When an authentic servant of God delivers the Word of God to the people of God, the Spirit of God can do his work in the lives of those people.

So I am asking you, pastor, to consider, as you wield this powerful weapon of the Spirit every week, whether and to what extent you are using it to bring your people a full understanding of God's redemptive plan as it relates to all creation. This kind of preaching takes sincerity, spiritual authenticity and courage. It may require you to challenge some of the opinions of those in your congregation. Tri Robinson, author of *Saving God's Green Earth,* waited years before he preached to his people about caring for God's creation, even though he knew God was calling him to do it. He admits that he was afraid of what the reaction would be. To his amazement, the reaction was a standing ovation. His fears were groundless. He need not have waited so long. Fear is not an acceptable reason for neglecting to preach the full word of God.

There are some disturbing parallels between the stand the church is willing to take now on environmental issues and the way previous generations of evangelicals wavered on the important questions of slavery and civil rights. It's obvious now that those pastors and churches who remained silent or who even actively opposed those issues were wrong. Embarrassingly wrong. Even tragically wrong. Let's not make the same mistake again.

Professor Wilson is right. As a pastor, you have a key role in the response to this crisis. May God give you grace—and courage—to play your part.

Dear Church Member,
You don't think you're anyone special. Just an ordinary Joe or Jane who sits halfway back in the sanctuary on the left-hand side. You love your Bible, but you may never have opened a book on theology in

your life. Your Christian life consists of being faithful in the little things. You pray for friends and relatives who are lost. You grieve when you hear about hungry people and orphans in other countries. You worry about your kids and grandkids and what kind of world is going to be left for them. But the environmental crisis seems too big. What can you do?

I encourage you to begin to make changes where you can. Little things make a big difference. Did you know, for example, that household water consumption in the United States has not increased for almost twenty years, even though our population has increased dramatically in that time? Do you want to know how? You were part of it: water-saving showerheads and low-flow toilets were mandated in many parts of the country in the late 1970s and 1980s. It doesn't seem like much, but the ten or twenty gallons saved on each shower multiplied by 300 million people is a lot of water. We saved enough collectively to accommodate millions more people with enough to go around. Few of us even noticed.

We need to do this in other areas. And we can. We don't have to wait for someone to tell us to reduce our electricity consumption by 10 percent (which is easy). Similarly we can reduce our driving. We can learn to purchase and consume less and use products that do less damage when we do use them. We can learn to walk lightly on this earth.

And we can speak up. Sometimes one voice at just the right time can make all the difference. You don't know how effective your one voice might be until you try. Let people know that you'd like to use something besides disposable dishes at church dinners. Encourage your pastor or Sunday-school leaders to teach creation care. See if your missions program is involved in an overseas creation-care project. Ask your office manager to buy recycled paper for the copier. Express your convictions about these things, and you'll find other people who feel the same way you do.

Did you know that 40 percent of the members of the Sierra Club are people of faith who attend worship services regularly? Tragically they hide their church membership while at Sierra Club meetings and their Sierra membership while at church. The result? Neither the Sierra Club nor the church reflects their views. You might be one of these. Speak up at both places, and discover how many friends you have.

Dear Student,

You've been on my mind all the way through this book. I was your age—or a bit younger, perhaps—when I was first touched by the environmental crisis on that first Earth Day in 1970. Many years slipped by before I picked up the topic again, or rather, before it found me, as I've already shared with you. I'm afraid you won't have the luxury of waiting for a decade or two. The crisis is upon us now, and it's serious.

Time is running out, but we're not without hope. If we, the human race, can take the appropriate steps now to manage our collective global affairs carefully for the next fifty or seventy-five years, we can navigate what Professor Wilson calls the bottleneck, but we have to begin now.

As Interstate 90 enters downtown Cleveland from the east, it runs along the shore of Lake Erie and then makes a sharp—and I do mean sharp—left turn to head south into the center of the city. On a highway where the speed limit is fifty-five miles per hour and most traffic goes sixty-five or better, a turn that can be navigated only at about thirty miles per hour is a major hazard. Traffic engineers know this, and so for a good two miles before that turn, they've installed some of the largest warning signs and flashing lights I've ever seen. The reason for all the warning signs is simple: if drivers slow down in time, they can manage the turn without difficulty or danger. If there were no warning signs, and drivers had to wait until they could see the turn to slow down, it would be too late to avoid a crash. The environmental trends we're seeing in the paper every day are like those warning signs, and the message is the same: SLOW DOWN NOW! Some leaders suggest that we should wait for more evidence. They want to actually see the bend in the road. If we wait that long, it really will be too late.

Our global civilization is racing toward such a turn. If you are a student now, you'll be at the height of your career when we hit the corner. You have an opportunity to make career decisions that will allow you to be among those who are stepping on the brake rather than the accelerator. What the world is crying for is leaders—people who will step up with knowledge (training), imagination and courage to guide our collective response to the environmental crisis. I would like to challenge you to be one of those leaders.

Our situation is as urgent as the Winter Race effort after the Pakistan earthquake, though it will play out over your entire career rather than the next six or seven weeks. You can have an impact in a host of fields. Scientists are needed who can work in the desperately short-handed fields of botanical and zoological taxonomy. We have to name many creatures so we know how to save them. (Talk about a divine mission: naming the creatures was one of Adam's first jobs.) We need political leaders and policymakers who will guide communities and nations in preserving God's creation, and business people who will lead the way in developing an economy that can feed and clothe the human race without destroying itself. More than anything else, we need pastors and church leaders who will make caring for God's creation the priority it must be. The church must be mobilized if any of the rest is to happen.

We don't choose the times in which we're born or the tasks that are presented to us. I wish that my own generation had made some different decisions along the way that would have made your task easier. Regretfully we didn't. But we can still move forward together.

All of us could do worse than to remember Elrond's words in J. R. R. Tolkien's *Fellowship of the Ring* as he addressed the Council just before Frodo agreed to carry the Ring to Mordor:

> *The road must be trod, but it will be very hard. And neither strength nor wisdom will carry us far upon it. This quest may be attempted by the weak with as much hope as the strong. Yet such is oft the course of deeds that move the wheels of the world: small hands do them because they must, while the eyes of the great are elsewhere.*[1]

Appendix 1

Mobilizing God's People
to Care for God's Creation

A Declaration for Action by Delegates of the Second International Conference on God and Creation
The following declaration was signed by more than two hundred church leaders from Kenya and twenty other countries on March 11, 2006, at Care of Creation's conference at Brackenhurst International Conference Center, Tigoni, Kenya. (See chapter five.)

As leaders and members of the evangelical church body in East Africa, representing a wide range of denominations and ministries, we stand together in agreement with the following declaration:

We believe in one God, the Creator, Owner, and Sustainer of all things, and we uphold the truth that His creation serves as a dynamic testimony of His power, wisdom, and glory.

As followers of Christ, we believe that God calls us to be good stewards of His creation. We embrace the truth that caring for creation brings glory to God, and that it serves as a practical expression of our love and concern for both current and future generations.

Upon reflection at this conference, we believe the environmental crisis emerging in East Africa poses a critical threat to our future. The creation is suffering as a result of deforestation, the degradation of agricultural and pastoral lands, pollution, the loss of biodiversity, and the greed of man. This is undermining the well-being of our communities and is leading to the impoverishment of our people.

We confess that the church has responded poorly to this issue. Our failure in promoting and exercising proper stewardship over the creation has undermined our witness for Christ, and we hereby declare that we repent of our sin and negligence in this matter.

Acknowledging that the Author of our salvation is also the Author of all creation (Jn 1:1-3 and Col 1:16), we also declare that, more than any other group of people, it is believers committed to sharing the love and truth of Christ who should take the lead in responding to this crisis. We believe that awakening the church to action is our most promising hope in the spiritual and physical battle against environmental degradation in the twenty-first century.

We therefore appeal to all church and denominational leaders to recognize the gravity of the situation and to begin developing God-centered strategies to educate, disciple, and mobilize the entire church to action. Our prayer is that God will initiate a powerful movement which will sweep across Africa and have an impact worldwide

As we join together in a spirit of humility and repentance, and begin taking the necessary action, we have reason for great hope! According to 2 Chronicles 7:14 this is the essential first step we must take if God is to bring healing to our land:

If my people, who are called by my name, will humble themselves and pray and seek my face and turn from their wicked ways, then I will hear from heaven and will forgive their sin and will heal their land.

Appendix 2

An Evangelical Declaration on the Care of Creation

Signed in 1994 by almost three hundred evangelical leaders, this document is the fruit of discussions begun at an Au Sable Institute Forum in August 1992 that led to a substantial report, "Evangelical Christianity and the Environment," and eventually to the formation of the Evangelical Environmental Network (EEN), now ably led by the Reverend James Ball. The story of the writing of this declaration and extensive commentary on the issues and theology behind it can be found in R. J. Berry, editor, The Care of Creation: Focusing Concern and Action *(InterVarsity Press, 2000).*

We have reprinted the document here because it is a significant evangelical statement on the issues addressed in this book and ought not to be lost, even in the dust of recent history, but also because it represents a good starting point for any church or evangelical organization seeking a concise theological platform from which to begin formulating its own response to creation-care issues. The full list of signatories can be found on the EEN website <http://www.creationcare.org/resources/signatores.php>.

The Earth is the Lord's, and the fulness thereof—Psalm 24:1
As followers of Jesus Christ, committed to the full authority of the Scriptures, and aware of the ways we have degraded creation, we be-

lieve that biblical faith is essential to the solution of our ecological problems.

Because we worship and honor the Creator, we seek to cherish and care for the creation.

Because we have sinned, we have failed in our stewardship of creation. Therefore we repent of the way we have polluted, distorted, or destroyed so much of the Creator's work.

Because in Christ God has healed our alienation from God and extended to us the first fruits of the reconciliation of all things, we commit ourselves to working in the power of the Holy Spirit to share the Good News of Christ in word and deed, to work for the reconciliation of all people in Christ, and to extend Christ's healing to suffering creation.

Because we await the time when even the groaning creation will be restored to wholeness, we commit ourselves to work vigorously to protect and heal that creation for the honor and glory of the Creator—whom we know dimly through creation, but meet fully through Scripture and in Christ. We and our children face a growing crisis in the health of the creation in which we are embedded, and through which, by God's grace, we are sustained. Yet we continue to degrade that creation.

These degradations of creation can be summed up as (1) land degradation; (2) deforestation, (3) species extinction; (4) water degradation; (5) global toxification; (6) the alteration of atmosphere; (7) human and cultural degradation.

Many of these degradations are signs that we are pressing against the finite limits God has set for creation. With continued population growth, these degradations will become more severe. Our responsibility is not only to bear and nurture children, but to nurture their home on earth. We respect the institution of marriage as the way God has given to insure thoughtful procreation of children and their nurture to the glory of God.

We recognize that human poverty is both a cause and a consequence of environmental degradation.

Many concerned people, convinced that environmental problems are more spiritual than technological, are exploring the world's ideol-

ogies and religions in search of non-Christian spiritual resources for
the healing of the earth. As followers of Jesus Christ, we believe that
the Bible calls us to respond in four ways:

First, God calls us to confess and repent of attitudes which devalue
creation, and which twist or ignore biblical revelation to support our
misuse of it. Forgetting that "the earth is the Lord's," we have often
simply used creation and forgotten our responsibility to care for it.

Second, our actions and attitudes toward the earth need to proceed
from the center of our faith, and be rooted in the fullness of God's revelation in Christ and the Scriptures. We resist both ideologies which
would presume the Gospel has nothing to do with the care of nonhuman creation and also ideologies which would reduce the Gospel
to nothing more than the care of that creation.

Third, we seek carefully to learn all that the Bible tells us about the
Creator, creation, and the human task. In our life and words we declare that full good news for all creation which is still waiting "with
eager longing for the revealing of the children of God" (Rom. 8:19).

Fourth, we seek to understand what creation reveals about God's
divinity, sustaining presence, and everlasting power, and what creation teaches us of its God-given order and the principles by which it
works.

Thus we call on all those who are committed to the truth of the
Gospel of Jesus Christ to affirm the following principles of biblical
faith, and to seek ways of living out these principles in our personal
lives, our churches, and society.

The cosmos, in all its beauty, wildness, and life-giving bounty, is the
work of our personal and loving Creator.

Our creating God is prior to and other than creation, yet intimately
involved with it, upholding each thing in its freedom, and all things
in relationships of intricate complexity. God is transcendent, while
lovingly sustaining each creature; and immanent, while wholly other
than creation and not to be confused with it.

God the Creator is relational in very nature, revealed as three persons in One. Likewise, the creation which God intended is a sym-

phony of individual creatures in harmonious relationship.

The Creator's concern is for all creatures. God declares all creation "good" (Gen 1:31); promises care in a covenant with all creatures (Gen 9:9-17); delights in creatures which have no human apparent usefulness (Job 39–41); and wills, in Christ, "to reconcile all things to himself" (Col 1:20).

Men, women, and children have a unique responsibility to the Creator; at the same time we are creatures, shaped by the same processes and embedded in the same systems of physical, chemical, and biological interconnections which sustain other creatures.

Men, women, and children, created in God's image, also have a unique responsibility for creation. Our actions should both sustain creation's fruitfulness and preserve creation's powerful testimony to its Creator.

Our God-given, stewardly talents have often been warped from their intended purpose: that we know, name, keep and delight in God's creatures; that we nourish civilization in love, creativity and obedience to God; and that we offer creation and civilization back in praise to the Creator. We have ignored our creaturely limits and have used the earth with greed, rather than care.

The earthly result of human sin has been a perverted stewardship, a patchwork of garden and wasteland in which the waste is increasing. "There is no faithfulness, no love, no acknowledgment of God in the land. . . . Because of this the land mourns, and all who live in it waste away" (Hosea 4:1,3). Thus, one consequence of our misuse of the earth is an unjust denial of God's created bounty to other human beings, both now and in the future.

God's purpose in Christ is to heal and bring to wholeness not only persons but the entire created order. "For God was pleased to have all his fullness dwell in him, and through him to reconcile to himself all things, whether things on earth or things in heaven, by making peace through his blood shed on the cross" (Col 1:19-20).

In Jesus Christ, believers are forgiven, transformed and brought into God's kingdom. "If anyone is in Christ, there is a new creation"

(2 Cor 5:17). The presence of the kingdom of God is marked not only by renewed fellowship with God, but also by renewed harmony and justice between people, and by renewed harmony and justice between people and the rest of the created world. "You will go out in joy and be led forth in peace; the mountains and the hills will burst into song before you, and all the trees of the field will clap their hands" (Isa 55:12).

We believe that in Christ there is hope, not only for men, women, and children, but also for the rest of creation which is suffering from the consequences of human sin.

Therefore we call upon all Christians to reaffirm that all creation is God's; that God created it good; and that God is renewing it in Christ.

We encourage deeper reflection on the substantial biblical and theological teaching which speaks of God's work of redemption in terms of the renewal and completion of God's purpose in creation.

We seek a deeper reflection on the wonders of God's creation and the principles by which creation works. We also urge a careful consideration of how our corporate and individual actions respect and comply with God's ordinances for creation.

We encourage Christians to incorporate the extravagant creativity of God into their lives by increasing the nurturing role of beauty and the arts in their personal, ecclesiastical, and social patterns.

We urge individual Christians and churches to be centers of creation's care and renewal, both delighting in creation as God's gift, and enjoying it as God's provision, in ways which sustain and heal the damaged fabric of the creation which God has entrusted to us.

We recall Jesus' words that our lives do not consist in the abundance of our possessions, and therefore we urge followers of Jesus to resist the allure of wastefulness and overconsumption by making personal lifestyle choices that express humility, forbearance, self-restraint, and frugality.

We call on all Christians to work for godly, just, and sustainable economies which reflect God's sovereign economy and enable men, women, and children to flourish along with all the diversity of creation. We recognize that poverty forces people to degrade creation in order to survive; therefore we support the development of just, free economies which empower the poor and create abundance without diminishing creation's bounty.

We commit ourselves to work for responsible public policies which embody the principles of biblical stewardship of creation.

We invite Christians—individuals, congregations, and organizations—to join with us in this evangelical declaration on the environment, becoming a covenant people in an ever-widening circle of biblical care for creation.

We call upon Christians to listen to and work with all those who are concerned about the healing of creation, with an eagerness both to learn from them and also to share with them our conviction that the God whom all people sense in creation (Acts 17:27) is known fully only in the Word made flesh in Christ the living God who made and sustains all things.

We make this declaration knowing that until Christ returns to reconcile all things, we are called to be faithful stewards of God's good garden, our earthly home.

Appendix 3

About Care of Creation, Inc.

Care of Creation is a **Christian environmental organization** seeking to awaken and mobilize the church to care for God's creation in the face of an environmental crisis that is already devastating vast areas of the world.

We are also **a missions organization**. We believe that environmental problems are sin problems, and we are convinced that the church of Jesus Christ is the world's best hope for dealing with this crisis.

We believe that **missions and care for God's creation belong together**.

We're about . . .
- **Loving God** by worshiping him in all we do;
- **Loving God's people** by sharing the good news we have in Jesus Christ and by strengthening and empowering local congregations to join in;
- **Loving God's world** by working with and through his people **to care for and heal God's hurting creation**.

We are at work . . .
- In **Kenya** through **Care of Creation—Kenya**, based at the Brackenhurst Conference Center in Limuru;
- In the **United States** through services and consultation through our **Madison, Wisconsin**, home office.

We invite you . . .

To partner with us by **supporting our work** with your prayers and your gifts. Care of Creation is a 501(c)(3) organization—all gifts are tax deductible. Donate on our website <www.careofcreation.org> or by mail at the address below.

To contact us for more information and who we are and what we do:

Care of Creation, Inc.
P.O. Box 44582
Madison, WI 53744
info@careofcreation.org
www.careofcreation.org
(608) 233-7048

Appendix 4

For Further Reading

Berry, R. J., ed. *The Care of Creation: Focusing Concern and Action.* Downers Grove, Ill.: InterVarsity Press, 2000.

Berry, Wendell. *The Art of the Commonplace: The Agrarian Essays of Wendell Berry.* Emeryville, Calif.: Avalon, 2002.

Bouma-Prediger, Steven. *For the Beauty of the Earth: A Christian Vision for Creation Care.* Grand Rapids: Baker, 2001.

———. *The Greening of Theology: The Ecological Models of Rosemary Radford Ruether, Joseph Sittler, and Jürgen Moltmann.* Atlanta: American Academy of Religion, 1995.

Brown, Lester R. *Plan B 2.0: Rescuing a Planet Under Stress and a Civilization in Trouble.* New York: Norton, 2006.

Bryson, Bill. *A Short History of Nearly Everything.* New York: Broadway Books, 2006.

Collins, Francis. *The Language of God: A Scientist Presents Evidence for Belief.* New York: Simon & Schuster, 2006.

DeWitt, Calvin. *Earth-Wise: A Biblical Response to Environmental Issues.* Grand Rapids: CRC Publications, 1994.

———, ed. *The Just Stewardship of Land and Creation: A Report of the Reformed Ecumenical Council.* Grand Rapids: Reformed Ecumenical Council, 1996.

Diamond, Jared. *Collapse: How Societies Choose to Succeed or Fail.* New York: Penguin, 2005.

Fortey, Richard. *The Earth: An Intimate History.* London: HarperCollins, 2004.

Friedman, Thomas L. *The World Is Flat.* New York: Farrar, Straus & Giroux, 2006.

Hall, Douglas John. *Imaging God: Dominion as Stewardship.* Grand Rapids: Eerdmans, 1986.

Hoezee, Scott. *Remember Creation: God's World of Wonder and Delight.* Grand Rapids: Eerdmans, 1998.

Louv, Richard. *Last Child in the Woods: Saving Our Children from Nature Deficit Disorder.* Chapel Hill, N.C.: Algonquin Books of Chapel Hill, 2006.

McDonough, William, and Michael Braungart. *Cradle to Cradle: Remaking the Way We Make Things.* New York: Farrar, Straus & Giroux, 2002.

McKibben, Bill. *Deep Economy: The Wealth of Communities and the Durable Future.* New York: Times Books, 2007.

Pearce, Fred. *When the Rivers Run Dry: Water—the Defining Crisis of the Twenty-first Century.* Boston: Beacon Press, 2006.

Robinson, Tri. *Saving God's Green Earth: Rediscovering the Church's Responsibility to Environmental Stewardship.* Norcross, Ga.: Ampelon, 2006.

Rodin, R. Scott. *Stewards in the Kingdom: A Theology of Life in All Its Fullness.* Downers Grove, Ill.: InterVarsity Press, 2002.

Schaeffer, Francis A. *Pollution and the Death of Man.* Wheaton: Tyndale House, 1970.

Schweiger, Larry. "A Call to Evangelicals to Join the Debate." *Creation Care Magazine,* Winter 2005, pp 10-12.

Sleeth, J. Matthew. *Serve God, Save the Planet: A Christian Call to Action.* White River Junction, Vt.: Chelsea Green, 2006.

Geisel, Theodor Seuss (Dr. Seuss). *The Lorax.* New York: Random House, 1971.

John Walton. *Genesis.* NIV Application Commentary. Grand Rapids: Zondervan, 2001.

Wilson, E. O. *The Future of Life.* New York: Knopf, 2002.

———. *The Creation: An Appeal to Save Life on Earth.* New York: Norton, 2006.

White, Lynn, Jr. "The Historical Roots of Our Ecologic Crisis." *Science* 155 (March 10, 1967): 1203-7.

Winter, Ralph. "The Uncertain Future of Missions." *Mission Frontiers,* March-April 2006, pp. 10-12.

Discussion Questions

Introduction

1. The author introduces himself as a "reluctant environmentalist." To what extent do you relate to this feeling? Do you find yourself more on the "reluctant" end of the scale or more on the "environmentalist" end? Why? How do you relate to people at the opposite end (p. 14)?

2. There is a tension between human responsibility and God's sovereign control of creation (and the fate of the environment). How do you respond to the sentence, "From our human perspective, the future of God's creation—and the human race—is in the hands of politicians, lawyers and teachers, businessmen and women, engineers and architects. Present and future pastors, teachers and ordinary Christians in particular hold the fate of creation in their hands" (p. 15)?

3. "Environmental problems are sin problems" (p. 18). We're going to explore this much more thoroughly in the chapters ahead. But think and discuss what this might mean, and how it affects how the church might respond to the environmental crisis.

Chapter 1

1. An invisible crisis (pp. 28-29)

   Some in your group may be old enough to remember the state of the environment before the Earth Day legislation of the early

1970s. Share some of your memories. And think about the implications of environmental problems that can't be seen. How might a problem's invisibility affect attitudes and a sense of urgency?

2. A population crisis (pp. 31-36)

   Explore the implications of a rapidly expanding human population. Do you agree that this is a particularly sensitive area for Christians? How do *you* balance the command to "be fruitful and multiply" (Genesis 1:29) with our obligations to love and care for each individual human being as someone "created in the image of God"?

3. A prosperity crisis (pp. 36-38)

   Think about the global airliner story. What kinds of "suitcases" are you bringing along? If it is true that we will not all be able to bring all we want—that is, we will not all be able to live the lifestyles we might want to live—due to the physical limits of our globe, what should we do? What should a Christian do? A traveler, faced with this kind of dilemma, has to prioritize. Can you think of some Bible passages that might apply here to help us decide what level of life style we should choose?

4. A poverty crisis (pp. 38-40)

   Some in your group may have visited countries like Haiti or Kenya. Share your experiences of seeing people in poverty. Think about the effects of dire poverty on the environment where such people live, and on God's creatures—plant and animal—that live in these places as well

5. A political crisis (pp. 40-42)

   Do you see the environmental stress behind the headlines of political crises you read about? Select one or two recent headlines from troubled areas of the world and explore together how these might have invisible—or even visible—environmental roots. Jared Diamond (p. 41) suggests that it is better to solve problems "in pleasant ways of our own choice" rather than allowing them to resolve themselves. What do you think he means? How might this principle apply to the stories you are discussing?

Chapter 2

1. "Who" matters (pp. 44-45)

   Jesus our Savior is God our Creator. Think about and discuss how this truth might affect how you think about God's creation. Does it change how you respond to a sunset or a beautiful flower in the woods? How about a foul and polluted stream?

2. "Why" matters too (p. 45)

   Did God create the world for us? Or for himself? Does the distinction matter? The author suggests that his concept of stewardship is richer and deeper because he knows God. Do you agree? How is this true for you? Explore some of the practical implications of this.

3. A temple carved out of space (pp. 46-50)

   Finding a balance between respecting creation and worshiping it has always been a challenge. Is it helpful for you to think of the world as a temple? What does that say about God's purposes in creating it? About how we should treat it? Have you had experiences of worship in God's creation that could not have happened in a church building (see p. 50)? Share some of these with each other.

4. The cosmic choir (pp. 50-53)

   If the purpose of our stewardship is "to help the cosmic choir to sing the heavenly song in the temple of creation" (p. 52), how should we respond to ongoing reports of species extinctions, loss of habitat for more and more of God's creatures, and similar developments? Discuss the statement "How do you think the choir sounds now that we've been sitting in the choirmaster's chair for thousands of years?" (p. 52). What is an appropriate response to God, the conductor of this choir, when we face this situation?

5. The book of God's works and the book of God's Word (pp. 53-55)

   Review Psalm 19 and notice that both of these "books" are discussed in this psalm. Discuss how we might learn to read both books together. If any members of your group are scientists (or students preparing for a scientific career), ask for their perspective on this. What does this concept say to someone who is a scientist? someone who is not a scientist?

Chapter 3

1. "When he came down he raised us up" (p. 57)

   How does the fact that Jesus the Creator walked on this earth affect how you think about the earth? about plants and creatures? about your fellow human beings? Discuss how Jesus' earthly presence extends the concepts that were explored in the previous chapter—the cosmic choir, the earth as a temple, etc.

2. "We should enjoy, but must not destroy, God's fruitfulness." (Cal DeWitt, p. 59)

   Discuss the tension inherent in this statement. Explore aspects of modern life that tend to destroy fruitfulness. Can you articulate some basic principles that would guide a person, a family or a community toward an enjoyment of fruitfulness that would not result in its destruction?

3. A carpenter, not a gardener (pp. 61-62)

   Environmentalism has sometimes taken the viewpoint that any human activity is bad for creation. How does Jesus' occupation as a carpenter counter that? Discuss the lessons we can take from this to help us find a balance in our own lives between respecting creation and taking from or using creation to fulfill our own needs.

Chapter 4

1. We didn't mean to (pp. 64-66)

   Do you agree that many sinful actions (environmental and otherwise) are not intentional? Are they still sin? Discuss how we can or should respond to the "unintended consequence" aspect of sin.

2. Relationships falling like dominoes (pp. 66-68)

   The author discusses four key relationships—human beings' relationship to God, to themselves, to each other and to creation.

(These will come up again when we discuss redemption.) Explore together how these relationships are interconnected. How does the breaking of one lead inexorably to the next? If environmental problems are in fact at the end of the chain, what does this say about what has to happen to solve the environmental crisis?

3. Sin and sinfulness (pp. 68)

Discuss the difference between *sin-as-something-one-is* and *sin-as-something-one-does*. Is this a new concept for you? Is it easier or more difficult to deal with one or the other? Using the MP3 player as an example, discuss ways in which a purchase can sometimes be sin and other times not. How might this change how you think about your next purchase of—anything?

4. The wages of (environmental) sin (pp. 69-70)

The author is suggesting that environmental problems are sometimes, literally, "the wages of sin." Do you agree? Read and discuss Isaiah 5:8-10. Apply these principles to some of the environmental situations that were described in chapter one or that you are aware of from recent news headlines.

Chapter 5

1. Reconciliation before restoration (pp. 73-74)

Colossians 1:15-20 is a key passage that undergirds this chapter and much of this book. Take some time to explore it together, noting in particular the repetition of the phrase "all things" and similar words. Compare this passage to the teaching of Romans 8:19-22. In what sense does Jesus' redemption apply to his nonhuman creation? How does it not apply? Are there implications here for how Christians should treat the nonhuman creation?

2. Putting the dominoes back in place (pp. 74-77)

Refer to the discussion of broken relationships in the last chapter (pp. 66-68), and discuss how the restoration of these interconnected relationships is similar to the way in which they were broken in the first place. Is it true that we are often satisfied with the restoration of just one or two of these relationships? Why do you think that is?

3. A peace that passes understanding (pp. 77-78)

Explore together the implications of the Hebrew concept of shalom as described in this chapter. Have you had shalom-type experiences that you can recall? Share them with each other. Discuss ways in which your present lifestyle encourages the development of shalom and ways in which it does not. How might you begin to move toward a way of living that gives you more shalom rather than less?

4. What about the rapture? (pp, 78-82)

"It's all going to burn up anyway!" is one of the most common—and silliest—objections raised by Christians to caring for God's creation. Do you agree with the author that whether the earth lasts or burns up is irrelevant to the question of what we do with it (p. 81)? How do your view of end times and the biblical promises of Jesus' return affect your commitment to care for his creation?

Chapter 6

1. Let the church be the church (pp. 84-86)

Review the author's story of the Mifflin Street Block Party and the way all four restored relationships are demonstrated in this incident. Share other stories you might recall of ways in which a church has taken this kind of initiative to make a difference in its community. Discuss why such incidents tend to be unusual. Do you agree with Wendell Berry (quoted on p. 87) that sometimes "salvation" is "really only another form of gluttony and self love"? How can we avoid this kind of mistake?

2. The church (local) and the church (universal) (pp. 87-88)

Discuss your understanding and your experience of the church as a local community of believers and the church as the universal, worldwide and throughout history "body of Christ." How do you personally keep these concepts together? The author says (p. 88) that the nature of the church is the central "hinge" of his argument that God's redemptive plan will be accomplished through his people. Explore this concept together. Do you think your fellow churchgoers see their church in this light? In what ways might this add significance to "ordinary" church activities?

3. Far as the curse is found (pp. 88-90)

The author suggests that God seems to have decided to allow us, the creatures who caused the curse in the first place, to be given the task of reversing its effects. "You broke it. I'm going to let you help me fix it" (p. 89). Discuss how this view of redemption is different from the "multilevel marketing" kind of redemption that he describes (pp. 89-90). What are the implications of such a view of the church?

4. A values-based organization (p. 90)

"Christians should care for creation more than anyone else because of what they already believe." Do you agree? Discuss this. What are some of the things that you already believe that influence how you think about or act toward God's creation? Why do you think many Christians do not act in accordance with their stated beliefs in this area?

5. A laboratory for community (pp. 91-93)

"The road back to environmental sanity takes us back to community" (p. 93). Do you agree that community tends to support environmentally friendly ways of living, and that aspects of life that diminish community also tend to be not so friendly to the environment? Why do you think this is? Discuss how the fact that the church is a community might enhance its impact on the environmental crisis.

6. A spiritual organism and a human organization (pp. 95-97)

The author suggests that the church is a "hybrid" (see pp. 96-97). What does he mean by this? Why does he think this makes the church the ideal, and maybe the only, human institution capable of responding to the fundamental challenges posed by the environmental crisis? Do you agree with this? Discuss the ways in which the environmental crisis is both human and spiritual, and how the human/spiritual hybridness of the church gives it a way to respond.

Chapter 7

1. Like a mighty army (pp. 101-4)

   Place your church fellowship on the line between the small fellowship in Kenya and a huge megachurch like Willow Creek or Saddleback. Review 1 Corinthians 1:26-29 (pp. 102-3) together. Does Paul's description of the Corinthians reflect how you and your fellow believers think of yourselves? (Be honest!) Discuss what Paul really means and how this passage applies to your church situation.

2. A challenge like no other (pp. 105-6)

   Read the refugee boat story together, and put yourselves in the position of the staff on that boat. How does the fact that the boat might be sinking affect how you would think about your own small assignment? Share your feelings and ideas. Apply them to the multifaceted ministries of your own church. How should people who are clearly called to ministries *other than* creation care think about and conduct their ministries in light of the environmental crisis?

3. When creation wins, everyone wins (pp. 106-7)

   The author claims that "becoming more creation-aware and more creation-caring always enhances other ministries in a church far more than it draws resources away from them" (pp. 106-7). The chapters that follow are going to build on this theme, but for now— do you agree? Does it make sense to you that this would be true?

Chapter 8

1. Creation-caring worship (pp. 108-9)

   "It appears that God hard-wired us to respond to him when we experience his world" (p. 108). Is this true in your experience? Share some ways in which you have "seen God" when experiencing his creation.

2. Singing and praying with creation (pp. 109-12)

Review the list of songs that have nature themes. You can probably add some of your own. Look over the list of suggestions for
incorporating more creation-care themes in worship. Discuss
these with regard to your own church. To what extent are they already being put into practice? How could your church improve in
this area? Here's a suggestion for action: bring these suggestions
to the folks who plan your worship services, and offer to help
them.

3. Preaching and teaching creation care (pp. 112-14)

Think about your own church's use of disposable cups and plates.
Changing this is an easy, visible way to make a difference—and to
save some money as well. The author appears to have a strong view
of the "power of the pulpit" (p. 111) to get people to change their
attitudes and behavior toward God's creation. Do you agree with
him? Why or why not? Have you heard many sermons on caring
for God's creation? Think about some you have heard and how they
affected you.

4. Reading two books together (pp. 114-15)

This is a recap of a theme that was also discussed at the end of chapter two. Explore how understanding that there are two books of
God's revelation might keep us from the error of worshiping creation rather than worshiping the Creator. "When we've been in error about God's creation, it has been because of too little time spent
in that book, not too much." Do you think this is true? Discuss
what can be done about it.

Chapter 9

1. The next generation (pp. 117-18)

Review together the life experiences of the three scientists: Calvin
DeWitt, E. O. Wilson and Francis Collins. Consider especially the
different paths they took toward (or away from) God. How might
things have ended up differently for any or all of them? Try to recall

some of your own early experiences growing up. What role does nature play in your earliest memories? To what extent did you (with or without the help of adults) connect these experiences with God?

2. Train a child in the way he should go (pp. 118-21)

If you have parents in your group, spend some time talking about how your kids relate to God's creation. What works? What doesn't? How is growing up today different than it was when you were kids? Richard Louv is quoted on page 121: "What does it mean when Sunday School begins to sound like Ecology 101 and environmentalists . . . begin to sound like street preachers? Good news for both of them." How is it good news for both?

3. Creation care in children's programs (pp. 122-27)

Review the list of suggestions for bringing creation-care themes into children's programs (p. 123) and for youth programs (p. 125). If any of your group are involved in Sunday School or youth group activities, discuss practical ways this list could be implemented in your church. What problems might you face?

4. Creation care at camp (pp. 127-30)

This section is of most interest to those involved in camping. Review the list of suggestions and compare it to your current programming. Think about the statement "If you could run your program in a gym, you're not using the resources and advantages God has given you." Discuss how to practically implement the suggestions given.

5. Creation care on campus (pp. 130-32)

If your group has college students, discuss the status of creation-care efforts on campus. Is there a recycling program? Does the institution seem to emphasize energy conservation? What can you as students do about it? Consider forming a creation-care student group—contact A Rocha (www.arocha.org) or Restoring Eden (restoringeden.org) for assistance.

Chapter 10

1. Godly and green (pp. 133-35)

   This chapter focuses on church facilities. Start off by walking around (literally or mentally) your church building and thinking about it in terms of God's creation. Does it "look" like it is friendly to creation? Does it feel that way? Why or why not? Is there evidence of creation concern—do lights get turned off, are there recycling bins?

2. Designing for worship (pp. 135-37)

   Think about your worship space. Are there windows? Can you see God's world while you worship? Can anything be changed to make creation more visible? If you can't open windows (because there are none), what can you do to bring nature inside? (PowerPoint slides don't count!)

3. Being energy stewards (pp. 138-40)

   Some aspects of energy conservation are visible and easy to implement—shutting off lights, turning off computers. But the real energy is used (and can be saved) in heating and air conditioning. Discuss how you can approach the people in charge of your church's facilities to review energy usage and to find ways to conserve.

4. Glorifying God on the grounds (pp. 140-43)

   As you did with your church building, take a walk (literal or in your mind) around your church grounds. Discuss with your group what you see: Is the property more "creature friendly" or more "car friendly"? What can you do to fix things up? Remember—there are lots of little things (bird feeders) as well as major landscaping changes that can make a difference. Review the list on pages 142-43 and talk about things you can do to implement some of these suggestions.

5. Inner-city churches (pp. 143-44)

   If your church setting is in an urban area where creation is harder to find, talk about your special needs and opportunities. Use the list (p. 144) to think about ways you can apply some of the principles of this chapter to your situation.

Chapter 11

1. The peace of our communities (pp. 145-46)

   Discuss how you feel about living in your town or city. Is your church a part of—or does it stand apart from—the rest of the community? Read Jeremiah 29:5-7 together and talk about what this means for you and your church. Does Jeremiah's command change the way you or your church think about or relate to the people you live and work with in your town?

2. My corner of God's creation (p. 147)

   The author gives a list of some of the environmental issues that face his community of Madison, Wisconsin. Take some time to make your own list for your town. In fact, make it a prayer list, along the lines of Jeremiah 29. Ask God to show you how you can love your community by tackling some of these problems.

3. Just being the church (pp. 148-49)

   Discuss this quote: "A church that's doing its job in terms of evangelism, discipleship and creation-caring, full-redemption teaching will be shaping the decisions [of people at work] more effectively than any store boycott or petition to Congress could do." What kinds of jobs do people at your church do? How could you (or others in your church) have an impact on the environmental crisis by a decision you make a work? Should a church dabble in politics when it comes to environmental issues (p. 149)? Discuss this in your group. How can a church have an influence on the outcome in areas like land-use policies that are clearly the job of the government but that also affect how creation-caring your community is?

4. Get your hands dirty (pp. 149-52)

   Loving our neighbors does mean getting our hands dirty. There are three categories of activities listed: creation appreciation (nature walks, for example), creation-healing (stream clean-up) and life-style transformation (bike to church). Discuss with each other the kinds of opportunities you might find in your community. Make a list under each category, and do one of each of them. Plan to talk with others in your church who plan outreach activities about including these kinds of activities in their plans.

5. Green evangelism (pp. 153-55)

The author encourages, but also warns about, using creation care as a means of evangelism. Review his concerns. How might "green evangelism" be seen as hypocritical by our neighbors? On the other hand, how might it be an effective "bridge to relationships"? Discuss ways to remain authentic and avoid the pitfall of hypocrisy in loving your neighbors through creation care.

Chapter 12

1. A healing mission (pp. 156-60)

The author recounts a conversation with a veteran missionary who wasn't sure how creation care would fit along with his idea of missions. And he says, "If the purpose of Christian missions or ministry is the accomplishment of this kind of full redemption, including creation care is not a distraction from the main goal. It is the goal" (p. 157). This may be a concern for some members of your group. Discuss the issue: Do you feel that including creation care as part of a missionary effort is a distraction from the main goal? Why? Why not? "Bad theology—or at least incomplete theology—will always give bad results" (p. 157). How was the theology of some early missionary efforts incomplete, according to the author? What kind of bad results is he reporting, for example, in Haiti or in Kenya? Do you agree that there is a connection between theology and results? Why or why not?

2. Theologically sound (pp. 160-62)

The author lists four aspects of a theologically sound missionary effort: biblically based plans, support of local church structures, informed staff teams and reliance on prayer. Discuss these and how they might affect a missionary effort you are familiar with. If there are members of your group with experience in missions, ask them how these things applied (or didn't) in their work.

3. Scientifically informed (pp. 162-65)

The comments in this section are of most interest to those actually involved in creation-care projects. If your group has people involved in planning or implementing such projects, review the suggestion list carefully. Would any of these ideas change the way your project is proceeding? Are there other suggestions you would include in this list?

4. Geographically comprehensive (pp. 165-67)

The author highlights a set of problems in Kenya that are all interconnected. Review these, and discuss how you might go about addressing such a complex set of issues. If you are in a group with people working on these kinds of projects, review the list of suggestions and consider how these might change the way you approach your own projects.

Chapter 13

1. And finally (pp. 168-69)

The author concludes the book with letters to three different groups of people: pastors, church members and students. You may want to read again the letter that seems most closely addressed to you, and discuss how you personally can respond to what you are being asked to do.

2. Dear Pastor (pp. 169-70)

The author feels strongly that pastors and church leaders in general have a key role to play in mobilizing the church. He bases this on what he calls "the unique power of preaching." Discuss this in your group. Do you agree with this? How can the tool of preaching be used most effectively in the church's response to the environmental crisis?

3. Dear Church Member (pp. 170-72)

   You are being asked to do some "little things"—and to "speak up" at church and at work. Discuss with your group what you are going to do as a result of this study. Make a list of "little things"—and then go home and do them. Think about ways that your one small voice might make a difference. And then use it!

4. Dear Student (pp. 172-73)

   You are in the unfortunate position of someone inheriting problems you didn't create. Discuss how this makes you feel? More or less inclined to get involved? Discuss how this study has influenced the way in which you look at your chosen career or field of study. Have you made (or will you be making) decisions in a different way than you did before?

5. And in conclusion (pp. 173-74)

   On the one hand, "what the world is crying for is leaders" (p. 173). On the other hand, "this quest may be attempted by the weak with as much hope as the strong" (Tolkien quote, p. 173). Discuss where you think you fall on this spectrum. Do you see yourself in a leadership role or as one of the quiet ones who influences things from the background? Discuss and pray together as you prepare to "mobilize the church."

Notes

Introduction

[1]E. O. Wilson, *The Creation: An Appeal to Save Life on Earth* (New York. Norton, 2006), p. 4.

[2]Lynn White Jr., "The Historical Roots of Our Ecologic Crisis," *Science* 155 (March 10, 1967): 1203-7.

[3]Ibid., p. 1205.

[4]Wilson, *The Creation*, p. 5.

Chapter 1: Running on Empty

[1]E. O. Wilson, *The Creation: An Appeal to Save Life on Earth* (New York· Norton, 2006), p. 29

[2]Frank Gilbreth Jr. and Ernestine Gilbreth Carey, *Cheaper By the Dozen* (New York: HarperCollins, 1948), pp. 2-3.

[3]See Janet Larsen, "Population Growing by 80 Million Annually," *Earth Policy Institute Eco-economy Updates*, 2002, <http://www.earth-policy.org/Indicators/indicator1.htm> (accessed October 9, 2007); United Nations, Department of Economic and Social Affairs, Population Division, "World Population Prospects: The 2006 Revision, Highlights, Working Paper No. ESA/P/WP.202," 2007, <http://www.un.org/esa/population/publications/wpp2006/WPP2006_Highlights _rev.pdf> (accessed October 9, 2007)

[4]Larsen, "Population Growing by 80 Million Annually."

[5]Thomas L. Friedman, *The World Is Flat* (New York: Farrar, Straus & Giroux, 2006), pp. 9, 10-11.

[6]World Wildlife Fund, "Living Planet Report 2006," <http://worldwildlife.org/news/livingplanet/pdfs/living_planet_report.pdf> (accessed October 9, 2007).

[7]Lester Brown, *Plan B 2.0: Rescuing a Planet Under Stress and a Civilization in Trouble* (New York: W.W. Norton, 2006). p. 10.

[8]A "bag" is a large burlap sack that would hold several bushels.

[9]See p. 26.

[10]Jared Diamond, *Collapse: How Societies Choose to Succeed or Fail* (New York: Penguin, 2005), pp. 498, 516, emphasis added.

Chapter 2: By Him and for Him

[1]John Walton, *Genesis*, NIV Application Commentary (Grand Rapids: Zondervan, 2001), p. 148.

[2]Quoted in Richard Louv, *Last Child in the Woods: Saving Our Children from Nature Deficit Disorder* (Chapel Hill, N.C.: Algonquin Books of Chapel Hill, 2006), p. 198, emphasis added.

[3]William Ted Johnson, "The Spiritual Lives of Great Environmentalists: John Muir, Calvin DeWitt," *Electronic Green Journal*, no. 24 (Winter 2006), <http://egj.lib.uidaho.edu/index.php/egj/article/view/3089/3047> (accessed October 19, 2007).

Chapter 3: The Divine Consumer

[1]James Jones, *Jesus and the Earth* (London: SPCK, 2003), p. 62.

[2]Ibid., p. 28.

[3]Calvin DeWitt, "Three Biblical Principles for Environmental Stewardship," *Au Sable Institute Online Resources*, <http://ausable.org/or.resources.online.7.cfm> (accessed October 19, 2007); and *Earth-Wise: A Biblical Response to Environmental Issues* (Grand Rapids: CRC Publications, 1994), p. 43.

Chapter 4: Diagnosis: Sin

[1]Jared Diamond, *Collapse: How Societies Choose to Succeed or Fail* (New York: Penguin, 2005), pp. 107, 114.

[2]Dr. Seuss, *The Lorax* (New York: Random House, 1971).

[3]David Roberts, "Materialism and Material," *Gristmill Blog*, August 17, 2005, <http://gristmill.grist.org/story/2005/8/17/151643/954> (accessed October 9, 2007).

[4]John DeGraaf, "AFFLUENZA: PBS Program on the Epidemic of Overconsumption," <http://www.pbs.org/kcts/affluenza/home.html> (accessed October 9, 2007).

[5]For a very good book-length exposition on these four key relationships, see Scott Rodin's *Stewards in the Kingdom* (Downers Grove, Ill.: InterVarsity Press, 2000).

Chapter 5: Reversing the Curse

[1]Stephen Bouma-Prediger, "God the Homemaker and Recycler: A Biblical Case for a Green God," Plenary address at MacLaurin Institute's Conference on Christianity and the Environment, September 23, 2006, <http://maclaurin.org/mp3s/stephen_boumaprediger.mp3> (accessed October 9, 2007).

Chapter 6: Ambassadors of Redemption

[1]Wendell Berry, *The Art of the Commonplace: The Agrarian Essays of Wendell Berry* (Emeryville, Calif.: Avalon, 2002), pp. 22-23.

[2]Ibid., p. 23.

Chapter 9: The Next Generation

[1]Amanda Leighhaaq, "Meet Calvin DeWitt: Environmental Evangelist," Lime.com, <http://www.lime.com/planet/story/4998/meet_calvin_dewitt_environmental_ evangelist> (accessed October 9, 2007).

[2]E. O. Wilson, *The Creation: An Appeal to Save Life on Earth* (New York: Norton, 2006), p. 144.

[3]Francis Collins, *The Language of God: A Scientist Presents Evidence for Belief* (New York: Simon & Schuster, 2006), p. 14.

[4]E. O. Wilson, *The Future of Life* (New York: Knopf, 2002), p. 146.

[5]Richard Louv, *Last Child in the Woods: Saving Our Children from Nature Deficit Disorder* (Chapel Hill, N.C.: Algonquin Books of Chapel Hill, 2006), p. 14.

[6]Louv, *Last Child*, p. 295.

[7]Patricia Fagg, "Ausable.org—Environmental Education Program, Great Lakes: Goals," <http://ausable.org/cp.gl.eep.goals.cfm> (accessed October 9, 2007).

[8]Cindy Crosby, "Christian Colleges' Green Revolution," *Christianity Today*, May 2007, <http://www.ctlibrary.com/45801> (accessed October 19, 2007).

Chapter 10: Godly and Green

[1]Neela Banerjee, "Citing Heavenly Injunctions to Fight Earthly Warming," *New York Times*, October 15, 2006, <http://www.nytimes.com/2006/10/15/us/15green .html> (accessed October 19, 2007).

Chapter 12. A Healing Mission

[1]Jared Diamond, *Collapse: How Societies Choose to Succeed or Fail* (New York: Penguin, 2005), p. 330.

Chapter 13: And Finally

[1]J. R. R. Tolkien, *The Fellowship of the Ring* (New York: Random House, 1965), p. 283.